NACOGDOCHES
FIRST BAPTIST CHURCH
NACOGDOCHES, TEXAS

Dedication

In the course of its 125-year history, twenty-two different men have served as pastor of the body of believers known as the First Baptist Church of Nacogdoches, Texas. Each of their ministries has left a significant legacy for the congregation and the community—some in facilities constructed, others in programs, still others in service rendered to the community and the denomination, but all in lives changed. To these, and especially to Dr. Allen Reed, who has shepherded this congregation for almost a third of a century, this book is dedicated.

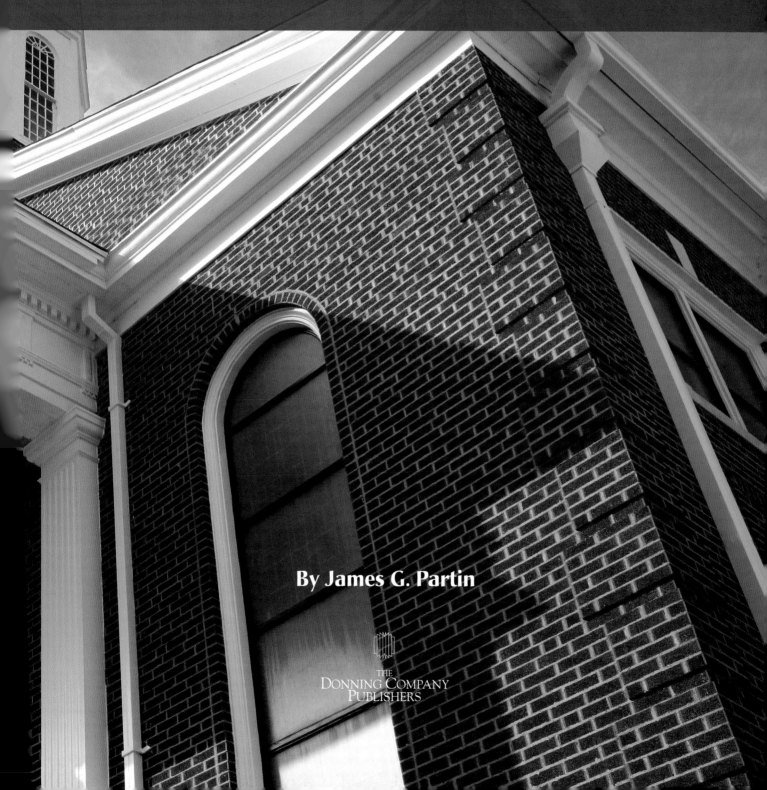

Advancing the Kingdom Since 1884
A Pictorial History of the First Baptist Church of Nacogdoches, Texas

By James G. Partin

THE
DONNING COMPANY
PUBLISHERS

The Donning Company Publishers
184 Business Park Drive, Suite 206
Virginia Beach, VA 23462

Steve Mull, General Manager
Barbara Buchanan, Office Manager
Pamela Koch, Senior Editor
Amy Thomann, Graphic Designer
Derek Eley, Imaging Artist
Cindy Smith, Project Research Coordinator
Tonya Hannink, Marketing Specialist
Pamela Engelhard, Marketing Advisor

Ed Williams, Project Director

Library of Congress Cataloging-in-Publication Data

Partin, James Gallaway, 1940–
    Advancing the kingdom since 1884 : a pictorial history of the First Baptist Church of Nacogdoches, Texas / by James G. Partin.
        p. cm.
    Includes bibliographical references and index.
    ISBN 978-1-57864-596-1 (hard cover : alk. paper)
    1. First Baptist Church (Nacogdoches, Tex.)—History. 2. Nacogdoches (Tex.)—Church history. I. Title.
    BX6480.N23P37 2009
    286'.17641820904—dc22
                                2009037283

Printed in the United States of America at Walsworth Publishing Company

Contents

Foreword

A Witness That Was Needed

In William Parmer's book, *Seventy-five Years in Nacogdoches: A History of the First Baptist Church*, we find these words about our town and our church:

> The town of Nacogdoches where there was not Baptist preaching at all . . . now has a Baptist church, and a spirit of progress in the work pervades the minds and enlivens the conversation of brethren and sisters in that town . . . There is no longer destitution in the town of Nacogdoches. She has a living church.[1]

Commitment to our Lord's Great Commission in Matthew 28:18–20 led our church's founding pastor and people to provide a witness to our community. They laid the groundwork that has made our church what it is today. For them and their dedicated witness, we are very grateful.

A Work That Is Ongoing

Faithful people throughout these past 125 years joined hands and hearts in working together to make our church what it is today. All are in agreement that while it took a joint effort by so many, it was actually the Lord God Himself who gave us the growth (1 Corinthians 3:6–9). For the spiritual and numerical growth that has taken place over the past 125 years, we are grateful.

A Watch That Is Continuing

Jesus is coming soon! That has been the watchword of Christians down through the centuries and continues to be for us as well. We don't know when our blessed Lord and Savior will return, but until He does it is our duty to "Work Till Jesus Comes." When the Lord does come, may He find us faithful in continuing the witness that

---

1. W. T. Parmer, *Seventy-five Years in Nacogdoches: A History of the First Baptist Church, 1884–1959* (Dallas, TX: Dorsey Co., 1959), p. 62.

was begun 125 years ago. May He find us working, witnessing, and watching. May our prayer ever be, "Amen. Even so, come, Lord Jesus!" (Revelation 22:20)

A Work That Is Acknowledged

This book is the work of many faithful members who love our church and whose desire has been to preserve our history in appreciation for what those of the past have done as well as for future generations.

A debt of gratitude is due to Jimmy Partin for his many hours of research and for the narrative he has written for the book. Likewise, our thanks to Rose Ann Pool, who has served as our 125th Anniversary Committee chairperson, and for all those who have served in any capacity to make the celebration of this anniversary possible. My personal appreciation goes to each of these and to the multitude of church members whose names will fill a list that stretches over 125 years. Our church is what it is today because of them.

Finally, our greatest expression of gratitude goes to our precious Savior, the Lord Jesus Christ. First Baptist Church of Nacogdoches is His Church. We are but stewards entrusted with the care of our people until He returns. May that be soon. All glory to "Him who is and who was and who is to come" (Revelation 1:4).

Allen Reed
First Baptist Church
Nacogdoches, Texas
January 2, 2009

Preface & Acknowledgments

*"The First Baptist Church of Nacogdoches has...
an ancient and honorable history."*

A. J. Holt
Pioneering in the Southwest

JANUARY 16, 2009, MARKED THE 125TH ANNIVERSARY OF THE BEGINNING of the First Baptist Church of Nacogdoches and of organized Southern Baptist work in the city. On this date in 1884, Luther Rice Scruggs, a graduate of Waco University and the Southern Baptist Theological Seminary in Louisville, Kentucky, was appointed by the Mt. Zion Baptist Association of East Texas to begin Baptist missionary work in Nacogdoches. As a result, First Baptist Church was organized sometime between May 7 and May 28, 1885. On May 7, the *Texas Baptist*, a denominational newspaper, stated that Scruggs expected to organize a small church in Nacogdoches soon. On May 28, the *Texas Baptist* reported that Scruggs had organized a church of thirteen members in Nacogdoches. This was the beginning of the church's "ancient and honorable history."[1]

Since that humble beginning, First Baptist Church has continued to minister to its members, to the city, to students of Stephen F. Austin State University, and to the world by fulfilling its mission of *Finding the Lost, Building the Believer, Changing the World.*

Dr. Allen Reed, who has served as the church's pastor for more than one-fifth of the time that First Baptist Church has existed, has had a long-standing goal of having a new history of the church to bring William Tellis Parmer's history of the church's first seventy-five years up to the present. Parmer's book, *Seventy-five Years in Nacogdoches: A History of the First Baptist Church, 1884–1959*, was published in 1959 to commemorate the congregation's seventy-fifth anniversary. Now the congregation has celebrated 125 years of formal witness to the saving power of

---

1. A. J. Holt, *Pioneering in the Southwest* (Nashville, TN: The Sunday School Board of the Southern Baptist Convention, 1923), p. 234.

Jesus Christ by Southern Baptists in Nacogdoches. It is in commemoration of that event that this volume is offered.

While I have relied heavily on Parmer's work for the first seventy-five years of the church's history, it was not my intent to replicate his scholarly and very complete treatise, but to provide a narrative history in an informal style that would appeal to a general audience while incorporating photographs and other illustrations that tell much of the story of First Baptist Church. Since biographies of the congregation's first seventeen pastors appeared in Parmer's book, the emphasis here has been to update those stories where appropriate and provide similar information within the narrative on pastors who have served since Parmer's book was published.

When work began on this project, an initial concern was that there might not be enough material and photographs to really tell the story of the church. I soon realized that just the opposite was true—there were almost too many documents and photographs to review and evaluate in the time available. The church archives stored in the vault and other places contain thousands of pages of minutes, reports, bulletins, letters, and financial data. There are more than 1,500 photographic slides, plus hundreds of black-and-white and color prints, many taken by Sherwood Lamkin, who served as the church's unofficial photographer for a quarter-century. Almost every week someone brought in more pictures or documents, frequently ones that I had not seen before. All together there is a great wealth of material, far more than can be used in the space available, so it was necessary to be highly selective and pick only images and information that would represent as broad a spectrum of people and events as possible. Regrettably, staying within reasonable limits on the number of pages and illustrations means that there will be people and events some will consider important in the life of the church that could not be depicted.

A selected bibliography lists the major sources consulted in the preparation of the manuscript. In keeping with the writing of a less formal history, endnotes are provided for direct quotations only. All other references may be found in the works listed in the bibliography. All photographs, unless credited otherwise, are from the archives of the First Baptist Church of Nacogdoches, Texas, and quotations from church members are from interviews conducted during the spring and summer of 2008.

A project of this magnitude is not accomplished without the help of many individuals. Of course, the danger in listing those whose contributions make a work possible, especially when a large number of individuals are involved, is that someone may be omitted inadvertently. With that in mind, I apologize to anyone whose contribution I have failed to acknowledge.

This pictorial history of the First Baptist Church of Nacogdoches is first and foremost the product of the vision of Dr. Allen Reed, the church's pastor for the past twenty-eight years. Without his gentle but constant prodding, the work might never have been completed. Likewise, the encouragement of Rose Ann Pool, who chaired the committees for planning both the 100th and 125th anniversary celebrations of First Baptist Church, was instrumental in bringing this project to completion.

A large debt is owed W. T. Parmer, whose *Seventy-five Years in Nacogdoches: A History of the First Baptist Church, 1884–1959*, published on the occasion of the seventy-fifth anniversary of the church's founding, provided the basis for most of the treatment of the church's first seventy-five years.

Members of the congregation, and townspeople as well, came forward with photographs, newspaper clippings, personal memorabilia, and remembrances that contributed in valuable ways to filling in gaps in the story.

The pastor's secretary, Emily Holden, graciously located and made available the church and deacon minutes as well as other documents. Pat Mullen, Anita Standridge, and Peggy Partin spent many hours collecting, sorting, and evaluating the large number of photographs in the church archives and those contributed by individuals. Without their assistance, identifying the pictures to include in this book would have been an almost impossible task. Likewise, Jackie Prince collected and organized many documents from the church archives and the offices of various church staff members, and Doyle Alexander sorted through and summarized a huge amount of budget data.

Jean and Johnny Rudisill, assisted by Nancy and Bob Dunn, interviewed numerous current and former church members, and the information they collected was a valuable aid in the preparation of the manuscript, as were the notes kept by Mary Cunningham, who served as Dr. Reed's secretary for twenty-one years.

Tom Atchison and Jonathan Canfield photographed a number of current events and buildings, and Canfield, the church's director of Media and

Communications, spent many hours using his technical skills to scan and edit the illustrations into electronic files for submission to the publisher. His expertise brought new life and clarity to many faded photographs and clippings.

Friend and colleague Dr. Archie McDonald lent his masterful skill as editor to provide valuable suggestions for improving the text, and Mrs. Portia Gordon, his assistant, worked magic with the computer to put the manuscript in the form requested by the publisher.

Pamela Koch and the staff of the Donning Company have kept the project moving and turned the photographs and text into a finished product.

Lastly, but certainly not least, my wife, Peggy, contributed not only her work on the project, her personal knowledge of the church's history, and her support, but frequently her patience with an author who sometimes became grumpy and irritable when the work was not going well. She and all those who contributed in so many ways to this project have my grateful appreciation. Any value it may have is largely due to their efforts. Any errors are mine alone.

1

A Living Church

"A live church exists in the town of Nacogdoches, with a good house, and with a pastor at a salary of $300, where only two years ago there was nothing."

Minutes of the Mount Zion Baptist Association, October 1886

THE INTRODUCTION OF CHRISTIANITY TO THE SPANISH PROVINCE of eastern Texas predated the beginning of Baptist work in the region by at least 125 years and the establishment of First Baptist Church of Nacogdoches by almost 200 years. It began with the establishment of Mission *San Francisco de los Tejas* near the Neches River by Father Damian Massanet in 1689. This effort was the first in a series of efforts of Spanish authorities to establish a string of missions, *pueblos*, and *presidios* to hold the eastern borders of New Spain against incursions from the East, first by the French and later by the Americans. The first mission established in what was to become the city of Nacogdoches was *Nuestra Senora de Guadalupe de los Nacogdoches*, founded July 9, 1716, by Father Antonio Margil de Jesus on the ridge between two creeks, probably not far from the future location of First Baptist Church.

Opposite: Adoniram Judson Holt, superintendent of missions for the Baptist General Convention of Texas, initiated Southern Baptist work among the Anglo population of Nacogdoches when he secured the appointment of Luther Rice Scruggs as Baptist missionary to the community. Holt later served First Baptist as pastor on two occasions. He is shown here at Union Baptist (Old North) Church, located about four miles north of Nacogdoches in 1936. *First Baptist Church Archives.*

Despite the best efforts of the friars, the East Texas missions were never successful at converting the native Caddo inhabitants of the region. The long overland supply route from San Antonio de Bexar meant that pay for the soldiers stationed at the *presidios* and supplies for both soldiers and priests arrived infrequently and in insufficient quantities. The scattered priests and soldiers did, however, hold eastern Texas for the Spanish crown and ensured that Nacogdoches would become the leading outpost of New Spain and later Mexico in the eastern part of the province. They also ensured that what religious practice existed in eastern Texas would remain almost exclusively Roman Catholic for the first two centuries of European occupation.

Roman Catholicism was the official religion of the Spanish Province of Texas and later the Republic of Mexico. Immigrants to the Mexican state of *Coahuila y Texas* were required to embrace the Catholic faith. Indeed, they could not become landholders or officeholders without doing so. Therefore, when Anglo immigrants began to filter across the largely unguarded borders of eastern Texas, those who reported to the authorities rather than bypass the entry points were asked to affirm that they were adherents to the Catholic faith. This resulted in numerous insincere conversions, such as Adolphus Sterne's migration from Judaism to Catholicism and Sam Houston's Catholic baptism in Sterne's front parlor. It also produced among the Anglo immigrants many nominal Catholics who subscribed to the faith in name only. W. T. Parmer observed in *Seventy-five Years in Nacogdoches* that this fiction of conversion to the Catholic faith produced "a sort of immunity against any form of organized religion"[1] on the part of the inhabitants of East Texas. This may, at least in part, explain why after the Constitution of 1836 guaranteed religious freedom in the Republic of Texas almost fifty years passed before Baptists established a congregation in Nacogdoches. Further evidence of the absence of religious practice was shown by Sumner Bacon's report to the American Bible Society in 1834 that only one in nine of the approximately six hundred American (Anglo) and three hundred Spanish families living in the area had a Bible. Bacon asked the Society to furnish him five hundred Bibles for immediate distribution, but there is no record of whether or not this was done.

Clandestine efforts at Protestant worship and fellowship occurred in eastern Texas prior to the establishment of the Republic of Texas. Families and individuals of a Protestant persuasion met in homes and sometimes

Luther Rice Scruggs, the first pastor of First Baptist Church, was a veteran of the Civil War who followed his preacher brother Thomas to Texas after the war. Assigned in 1884 by the Baptist General Association of Texas to initiate Baptist missionary work in Nacogdoches, Scruggs organized the first Southern Baptist church in the town by the end of that year. *First Baptist Church Archives.*

in the open air for prayer and worship. Beginning in 1834, Mrs. Massey Sparks Millard conducted prayer meetings under a large oak tree about four miles north of Nacogdoches. Several Methodist, Baptist, and Presbyterian ministers also preached and held meetings in the area between the Sabine River and Nacogdoches, ready to flee across the river when pressured by Mexican authorities. Shortly after the Texas Revolution, Isaac Reed, a Baptist minister, observed that prior to Texas independence, "It would probably have cost a man his life to have preached other than Catholic doctrine so near to Nacogdoches, the then headquarters of Mexican authority in eastern Texas."[2] Enforcement of the law may not have been so strict as Reed thought because a report to Mexican authorities in San Antonio early in 1831 stated that the *ayuntamiento*, or town council of Nacogdoches, had "received as citizens" seventy-two "strangers" of whom twenty-seven were of "different religions," meaning they were not Catholic.[3]

The first documented Baptist sermon to be preached in the city of Nacogdoches was delivered by a Baptist preacher from Tennessee, Z. N. Morrell, on Sunday, January 10, 1836, while an election was taking place. Morrell related that while traveling toward the town his "very soul burned within [him] to preach Jesus."[4] Upon arriving, he discovered the foundation timbers of an unfinished building, used them for pews and pulpit, and preached to the crowd that gathered to hear him.

After Texas achieved independence, Protestants, including Baptists, were quick to organize congregations and establish churches. On the first Sunday in May 1836, Isaac Reed and Robert E. Green organized Union Baptist Church, later known as Old North Church, in a log schoolhouse located about four miles north of the town of Nacogdoches. This church was a direct outgrowth of the prayer meetings held earlier under a large oak tree at that spot by Mrs. Massey Sparks Millard. Other congregations in Nacogdoches County were soon organized, such as Hopewell, a primitive, or "hard shell," Baptist church established September 17, 1837, at Cook's Settlement near present Douglass. Almost another fifty years passed, however, before a Baptist congregation was organized in the town of Nacogdoches proper.

After the Texas Revolution, the newly established Baptist congregations in East Texas lost little time in forming local associations. In 1839 the Union Association of Regular Predestinarian Baptist Faith and Order was organized by a group of Baptist congregations from several East Texas counties, including Hopewell Baptist Church in Nacogdoches County. Controversies over predestinarianism and mission work rocked the meetings of this early association, resulting in the establishment of other associations of Baptist congregations. In 1843, Union (Old North) Church hosted the organizational meeting of the first missionary Baptist

"I PASSED THROUGH SHREVEPORT AND NACOGDOCHES. THAT WAS MY FIRST SIGHT OF THE OLD TOWN OF NACOGDOCHES WHERE SO MUCH OF MY MINISTRY WAS AFTERWARDS SPENT. IT WAS . . . A SMALL TOWN OF POSSIBLY 800 PEOPLE. IT HAD ONLY ONE CHURCH AND THAT WAS CATHOLIC, AS I NOW RECALL."

A. J. Holt, 1870

Communion Service

According to tradition, this is the original communion service used by First Baptist Church. It was rescued by Frances (Mrs. John) Rudisill from the kitchen of the wooden church building designed by Diedrich Rulfs just before the building was demolished in 1941. Mrs. Rudisill kept the service in her home until the new brick church was finished and then placed it in the church library. When that building was destroyed by fire in 1953, Mrs. Rudisill rescued the service a second time, bringing it out of the burned building, smudged but intact. It has been displayed in the church parlor and, most recently, on the mantle of the Fireside Room where it serves as a reminder of the long history of First Baptist Church and of the importance of the ordinance of the Lord's Supper. *Photo by Jonathan Canfield.*

association in East Texas, the Sabine Baptist Association. Among the organizing congregations of this association were two Nacogdoches County churches, Union (Old North) and Mount Zion. Within three years this association included sixteen congregations with a total of 527 members. Soon it, too, was torn by controversy over missions and split into three factions at its fifth annual meeting in 1847.

Two years later, Union (Old North) Church again hosted an organizational meeting for a new Baptist association, the Eastern Texas Association of United Baptists that became the Central Baptist Association in 1852. Two Nacogdoches County Baptist churches, Union and Melrose, joined this association. In 1857, thirteen Nacogdoches, Panola, and Rusk County Baptist congregations pulled out of the Central Baptist and Sour Lake associations to form the Mount Zion Association of Missionary Baptists in East Texas. Union (Old North) Church took part in the organization of this new association, and New Salem Baptist Church of Nacogdoches County soon joined them. The pastor of Union (Old North) Church, B. E. Lucas, was a member of the Mount Zion Association Committee on Domestic Missions. It was the work of this committee that, twenty-six years later, established the mission program in Nacogdoches that resulted in the organization of First Baptist Church.

Following the Civil War, an upsurge of evangelism swept the Southern states and soon reached Texas. In 1871 the Baptist State Convention of Texas submitted a resolution to the Southern

Baptist Convention requesting the appointment of an individual to represent the interests of the Foreign Mission Board and the Domestic Board in overseeing mission work in Texas.

In 1882, the Baptist General Association of Texas appointed Adoniram Judson Holt as the first superintendent of missions for the state. The Baptist General Association of Texas and the Southern Baptist Convention jointly supported him, and he immediately began to establish missionary work in Texas communities where no Baptist congregations existed, including Nacogdoches. When he passed through Nacogdoches in 1870, Holt estimated the population at approximately eight hundred people with no organized Baptist church, a small congregation of about twenty-three Methodists, a small Episcopal congregation without a resident priest, and a Catholic church with declining influence, despite the presence of an estimated several hundred Mexican Catholics in the county. Holt also observed that many of Nacogdoches' leading male citizens belonged to a Liberal League that "leaned toward atheism"; others said the town had a saloon on every corner, as many as thirteen at one time. It was also a town that was on the verge of economic growth. The Oil Springs oilfield, located in the southeastern part of the county, near Woden, was under

North Street looking north, c. 1903. First Baptist Church is located on the left. The wooden front steps of the building Diedrich Rulfs designed for the church can be seen at the extreme left of the picture. The church has occupied this location continuously since 1885. *First Baptist Church Archives.*

The first building of First Baptist Church was constructed during the pastorate of L. R. Scruggs in the spring of 1885 on the location of the present auditorium. A. B. Vaughn was the last pastor to serve in this building. This watercolor sketch was painted by Dr. George L. Crocket, rector of Christ Episcopal Church in Nacogdoches. Dr. Crocket gave it to Mrs. Robert Lindsey, who in turn presented it to the church. *First Baptist Church Archives.*

development, and the arrival of John Paul Bremond's Houston, East and West Texas Railroad in 1883 provided transportation for goods and produce to Shreveport and Houston.

Holt was "determined to end gospel destitution" in Nacogdoches.[5] He prevailed upon the Mount Zion Baptist Association to adopt a resolution requesting the Baptist General Association of Texas to share the cost of a missionary in Nacogdoches on an equal basis with the Mount Zion Association. At Holt's urging the Association appointed Luther Rice Scruggs, a recent theology graduate of Waco University and Southern Baptist Theological Seminary, to begin the Baptist missionary work in Nacogdoches. Scruggs arrived in Nacogdoches early in 1884 to find a town still considered the "Catholic head quarters of East Texas."[6] The field, Scruggs reported shortly after his arrival to the *Texas Baptist*, a denominational newspaper published in Dallas, was "now white for the Baptists" to reap a harvest.[7]

When Scruggs arrived in Nacogdoches, he found twenty-six professing Baptists but no organized Baptist church. He reported to the *Texas Baptist* that the most pressing need was for a building in which to conduct services. He estimated the cost of an appropriate structure at $1,500. Within five weeks he collected almost $500, including a contribution from the *Texas Baptist* and $50 given by an Episcopalian. At the end of eight and one-half months, Scruggs reported to the annual meeting of the Mount Zion Baptist Association that he had traveled 2,008 miles, preached seventy-eight sermons, organized one church (Trinity Baptist, located four miles east of Nacogdoches), performed thirty-two baptisms, and distributed two thousand tracts in his 258 days on the job. Still, there was no building for the little group of Baptist believers in Nacogdoches. At this meeting the Mount Zion Association reappointed Scruggs as missionary to Nacogdoches, "with the privilege of traveling among the churches and soliciting assistance to build a church house at Nacogdoches."[8]

In February 1885, A. J. Holt, superintendent of missions for the Baptist General Association of Texas, assisted Scruggs with a revival in Nacogdoches. He brought with him a "little baby organ" for use in the services.[9] One source placed the services in a schoolhouse, and another said that they gathered in the Methodist Church building. Regardless of its location, the meeting resulted in twenty-one conversions, according to Lelia Orton (Mrs. John Lucas), one of the converts. Mrs. E. L. Martin, Orton's sister, wrote in her diary that the new converts were baptized in the chilly waters of Banita Creek, at a site just north of the Main Street crossing, on a cold February day with a freezing mist falling. These, along with at least some of the twenty-six Baptists Scruggs had found on his arrival in Nacogdoches, formed the nucleus of the church he organized sometime between May 7 and May 28, 1885. On May 7, the *Texas Baptist* reported that Scruggs anticipated organizing a church in Nacogdoches soon. Three weeks later, the *Texas Baptist* reported that Scruggs, along with two elders from Rusk County and Elder L. R. Heflin of Nacogdoches County, had organized the "first Baptist church in this old priest ridden town" with an initial membership of thirteen.[10] Although Scruggs referred to the church he organized as the *first* Baptist church organized in Nacogdoches, it would be more accurate to describe it as the first *Southern* Baptist church in the town, because five years earlier the Reverend Lawson Reed, an African American Baptist minister, organized Zion Hill First Baptist Church with twelve individuals who "presented themselves as Baptist candidates" in a revival he conducted.[11]

On October 3, 1885, First Baptist Church was received into the fellowship of the Mount Zion Baptist Association at its annual meeting held at Union (Old North) Baptist Church. The Association's minutes stated that

"WE TOOK ADVANTAGE OF THE PRESENCE OF THE BRETHREN [*SIC*] NAMED ABOVE [ELDERS HAYES, ISBELL, AND L. R. HEFLIN] AND ORGANIZED THE FIRST BAPTIST CHURCH IN THIS OLD PRIEST RIDDEN TOWN OF 13 MEMBERS. OTHERS WILL JOIN SOON."

Luther Rice Scruggs

Original Organ of First Baptist Church

On the side of this organ is a brass plaque that reads:

**ORIGINAL ORGAN OF
FIRST BAPTIST CHURCH
NACOGDOCHES, TEXAS
PURCHASED IN 1885
RESTORED IN 1955 BY
MR. EDGAR EDDINGS**

Oral tradition of the Ezra Prince family says that this is the original organ of First Baptist Church and perhaps is the "little baby organ" that A. J. Holt reported he brought to Nacogdoches in February 1885 when

he assisted with a revival conducted by the Reverend L. R. Scruggs. Holt was the superintendent of missions for the Baptist General Convention of Texas, and Scruggs was the Baptist missionary assigned to Nacogdoches. It was partially as a result of this revival meeting that the church was formally organized later that spring.

Prince family tradition states that the organ was stored at the church after it was replaced, possibly by the electric organ purchased for the new brick sanctuary constructed in 1942. Later it was loaned to the Baptist Student Union, and BSU director Bill Coble had it taken to Pops Lake where it was used for BSU retreats. When Coble's successor, Jimmy Wray, moved the location of the BSU retreats to Pineywoods Baptist Encampment near Woodlake, Texas, the directors of the Pops Lake Club asked Ezra Prince to remove the organ. Jared Cartlidge, pastor of First Baptist at the time, told Prince "to do whatever he wanted with it, as by now it was in bad repair. I think he assumed that it would be junked. Daddy [Ezra Prince] put it in our storage room behind the garage on North Street. Jerry [Prince] and I [Jean Prince Reese] spent many a happy hour playing and singing hymns and playing 'church.' When in later years the organ was completely beyond playing, Daddy was going to take it to the dump, but Uncle Edgar [Eddings] heard about it and asked if he could have it to fix up. Daddy delivered it to his garage in the back of a 7UP [Bottling Company] truck."[1] Eddings restored the organ, even whittling replacements for missing decorative parts. It remained in the possession of Mrs. Edgar (Ina) Eddings until she stopped housekeeping and moved into Hotel Fredonia. At that time she gave it to her nephew, Jerry Prince, son of Ezra Prince. It is now in the home of Prince's widow, Jackie Prince of Nacogdoches, Texas. *Photo courtesy of Jackie Prince.*

---

1. Jean Prince to Jackie Prince, email February 6, 2009.

"There is no longer destitution in the town of Nacogdoches. She has a living church. Let her choose a pastor, make known what they can pay toward his support, and petition this body and the General Association to pay what they lack."[12]

Although formally organized as a church, the congregation still had no place to meet. According to tradition, the body met at times in a small school, the Methodist meetinghouse, and sometimes in the open air while waiting for their own building. One possibility investigated was constructing a dual-purpose facility in cooperation with Milam Lodge No. 2, Ancient Free and Accepted Masons. This investigation proceeded so far as the lodge appointing a committee to study the feasibility of such an effort. After the lodge rejected a motion to build a lodge hall in connection with the church, the congregation pursued other possibilities. On December 31, 1885, church trustees C. W. Jones and J. H. Sutton purchased a lot on North Street, originally owned by Frost Thorne, from Julia Curl and Anna M. and J. C. Shindler. Construction of a one-room frame building in which to conduct services must have begun immediately, because by June 30, 1886, the structure was completed at a cost of $950 for both building and lot. A white, wood frame structure with a steeple rising above a columned porch, the building featured double front doors and five windows on each side. One early member recalled the building as not "ceiled" [sealed] and painted until the pastorate of W. M. Gaddy (1886–1890). Painted and sealed or not, it served the needs of the congregation for fourteen years.

With a meetinghouse in place, Scruggs and the new congregation turned their attention to growing the membership and establishing a firm foundation for the church. The congregation sent representatives to the first annual session of the newly organized Baptist General Convention of Texas in Waco, June 29–July 2, 1886. Scruggs, along with W. H. Wood and W. L. Pierce, served as messengers to the convention from the Nacogdoches body, bringing with them the church's contribution of $1.25 to the convention. Scruggs also submitted the combined contributions of all the churches in the Mount Zion Association, which amounted to a total of $29.40.

Scruggs' ministry in Nacogdoches lasted for almost three years. In September 1886, he left Nacogdoches to serve as a missionary in Dallas County. In his last report to the Mount Zion Association as pastor of First Baptist, Scruggs stated that

In 1879 the Reverend Lawson Reed, an African American Baptist minister, organized Zion Hill First Baptist Church with thirteen converts from a revival he preached. Zion Hill was the first organized Baptist congregation in the city of Nacogdoches, and Reed served as its pastor for approximately twenty-five years. This Gothic-style building, located on North Lanana Street, was designed for the congregation by noted Nacogdoches architect Diedrich Anton Wilhelm Rulfs in 1914. *East Texas Research Center, Stephen F. Austin State University.*

during the past year he had traveled 3,007 miles, made 564 family and religious visits, preached seventy-five sermons, received thirty-one individuals by church letter and fifteen on confession of faith, distributed two thousand religious tracts, and organized one Sunday school. At the end of his tenure in Nacogdoches, the Mount Zion Association paid tribute to Scruggs by stating that "A live church exists in the town of Nacogdoches, with a good house, and with a pastor at a salary of $300, where only two years ago there was nothing. This labor has been rendered by Brother Scruggs."[13]

In the fall of 1886, William Gaddy was called to pastor the fledgling Nacogdoches congregation. Under Gaddy's leadership the church began its long association with youth work when it became one of only eight congregations in the state to have a unit of the Christian Co-Laborer's Society, an organization with the stated purpose of promoting the spiritual development of youth. Later, in 1890, the name of this organization was changed to the Baptist Young People's Union. Giving to mission work also increased during Gaddy's pastorate, evidenced by an increase in the congregation's annual mission contributions to the Mount Zion Association. In 1890 the church sent $70 for home missions and $5 for foreign missions with Gaddy to the annual associational meeting. The significance of this amount may be seen when compared to the $1.25 that Scruggs conveyed to the state convention on behalf of the congregation only the year before.

Before his conversion, Gaddy worked as a saloonkeeper in Mt. Enterprise, Texas, so he did not hesitate to enter such establishments in Nacogdoches to witness to the patrons he found there. As Nacogdoches hosted a dozen or more such establishments, Gaddy did not lack for opportunities to try to reform whiskey drinkers. No record exists of any conversions resulting from these efforts, but the congregation did grow significantly under Gaddy's leadership. The church records show that membership increased from thirty-seven at the beginning of his pastorate in 1886, to ninety-seven at its conclusion in 1889. Some of this growth may have been the result of two revival meetings held at the church by A. J. Holt during this period. While conducting one of these meetings, Holt discovered that a Liberal League whose membership included "the brainiest men of the town" and several county officials was meeting each Sunday, and he aimed a series of messages specifically at its members. The conversion and subsequent testimony of one of the League's members caused a revival to break out in the entire town that lasted for the next six months, resulting in a number of additional conversions.

Gaddy resigned the Nacogdoches pastorate late in 1890. Before he left, the congregation changed its associational membership from the Mount Zion Association to the Nacogdoches Baptist Association on September 27, 1890. This Association, which had formed in 1886, was composed of twenty-seven Nacogdoches County congregations in addition to First Baptist, plus two from Angelina County. Initially the Nacogdoches Association was not as "missionary minded" as the Mount Zion Association, but the influence of First Baptist caused it to become more committed to mission work, a trend that continues.

1. W. T. Parmer, *Seventy-five Years in Nacogdoches: A History of the First Baptist Church, 1884–1959* (Dallas, TX: Dorsey Co., 1959), p. 22.

2. Willie Earl Woods Tindall, "Religion: Recollections & Reckonings," *The Bicentennial Commemorative History of Nacogdoches* (Nacogdoches Jaycees, 1976), p. 91.

3. Parmer, *op. cit.*, p. 21.

4. Tindall, *op. cit.*, p. 88.

5. A. J. Holt, *Pioneering in the Southwest* (Nashville, TN: The Sunday School Board of the Southern Baptist Convention, 1923), pp. 55–56.

6. Parmer, *op. cit.*, p. 55.

7. Ibid., p. 57.

8. Ibid., p. 59.

9. Ibid.

10. Ibid., p. 60.

11. Tindall, *op. cit.*, p. 94.

12. Parmer, *op. cit.*, p. 62.

13. Ibid., p. 64

"THE TOWN OF NACOGDOCHES, WHERE THERE WAS NO BAPTIST PREACHING AT ALL UNTIL THIS BODY SENT AS A MIS-SIONARY, BROTHER L. R. SCRUGGS . . . NOW HAS A BAPTIST CHURCH, AND A SPIRIT OF PROGRESS IN THE WORK PERVADES THE MINDS AND ENLIVENS THE CONVER-SATION OF BRETHREN AND SISTERS IN THAT TOWN."

Minutes of the Mount Zion Baptist Association

2

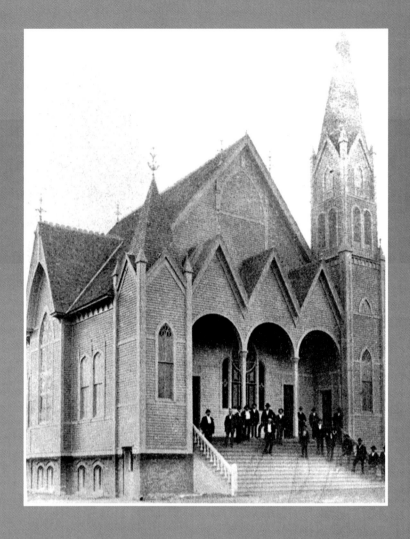

Building Up the Waste Places

*"I . . . was minded to use that time building
up the 'waste places' in Zion."*

Adoniram Judson Holt
Pioneering in the Southwest

FOLLOWING GADDY'S RESIGNATION IN 1890, FIRST BAPTIST extended a call to Adoniram Judson Holt, director of missions for the Baptist General Association of Texas. Holt had been responsible for securing the appointment of Scruggs as missionary to Nacogdoches and held revival services at the church. He learned of the invitation while attending the Southern Baptist Convention in Birmingham, Alabama. At about the same time, Holt also received a call to pastor First Baptist Church of Houston, Texas. The Nacogdoches church paid a salary of $800 for half time while the Houston church offered $2,500 for a full-time position. In spite of the much lower salary, Holt felt led to accept the call of First Baptist Nacogdoches because of his previous work there, and, as he stated in his autobiography, he had a desire to work in "building up the 'waste places' in Zion."[1] Mrs. E. L. Martin (Zula Orton) recorded in her diary that before Holt agreed to accept the call to Nacogdoches, he required the church to pay the back salary owed his predecessor, a move likely designed to ensure that the congregation would take its financial obligations to its pastor more seriously in the future. This would be the first

Opposite: The second building constructed by First Baptist was designed by Diedrich Rulfs and completed in 1900 on the site of the original church building. *First Baptist Church Archives.*

Diedrich Rulfs was the architect of the second building constructed by First Baptist. Rulfs, a German immigrant, designed more than fifty structures in Nacogdoches, Lufkin, Garrison, San Augustine, and Crockett. Two examples of Nacogdoches churches he designed are still standing, Zion Hill First Baptist Church, on North Lanana Street, and Christ Episcopal Church, on the corner of Mound and Starr streets. *First Baptist Church Archives.*

Right: This interior view of the auditorium of the building designed by Diedrich Rulfs shows the pulpit from the building that is used by the church in its lower auditorium. The woodwork behind the pulpit is similar to that in Zion Hill First Baptist Church, also designed by Rulfs. The baptistery was located underneath the platform and was accessed by moving the pulpit and taking up the platform floorboards. *First Baptist Church Archives.*

of two pastorates served at First Baptist by Holt. One of the most popular pastors in the early days of the church, Holt, in time, received a total of five invitations to shepherd the church.

Holt began his "building up of the cause in all of East Texas" by editing and publishing a religious newspaper he called *A Voice in the Wilderness.*[2] He invited ten men he considered among the best available preachers to conduct a two-week Minister's Institute at First Baptist focusing on what he called practical theology. There were morning and afternoon sessions for the preachers attending and an evening sermon open to the public delivered by the day's featured lecturer. One of the lecturers, Dr. J. M. Carroll, commented that the institute was "the greatest blessing that had to that time come to the East Texas Baptist ministry."[3]

Always active in denominational affairs, Holt persuaded First Baptist to host the fifth annual session of the Nacogdoches Baptist Association in September 1891, and he preached the annual associational sermon on missions. The report submitted by First Baptist to the Association that year showed membership increased to eighty-eight, the church owned property valued at $1,200, and a contribution of $72 each was made to state and foreign missions. Not surprisingly, given Holt's background, mission work was a strong emphasis for the congregation, as indicated by the mission offering at the associational meeting that included a pledge from First Baptist for an additional $50 to be sent later. June C. Harris, a former member of the Liberal League who was converted by Holt in the revival held during Gaddy's pastorate, was listed in the report as serving as church clerk. Membership continued to grow under Holt's leadership, and the associational report for the following year showed a net increase in membership of twenty-eight, with eighteen baptisms and twenty-four additions by letter.

In 1893, Holt resigned to accept a call from the First Baptist Church of Palestine,

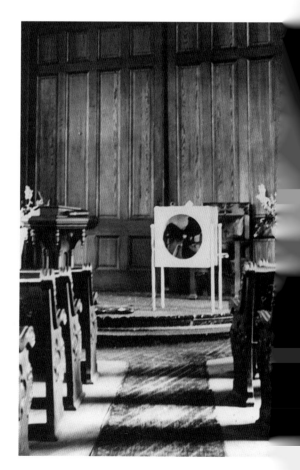

Texas. The decade following his first pastorate in Nacogdoches witnessed a procession of four pastors in rapid succession at First Baptist, but the little congregation continued to grow and prosper.

Herman Boerhave Pender, considered a strict disciplinarian and one of the leading pulpiteers of East Texas at the time, succeeded Holt as pastor of First Baptist. During his brief, two-year pastorate (1893–1895), the congregation received thirty-six members by baptism and fourteen by transfer of membership. The total annual contributions for all missions, associational, state, and foreign, grew to $135, but the salary paid the pastor remained $800, the same as paid when Holt was called but still $500 more than was paid to Scruggs.

Thomas Bunyan Harrell served one of the shortest tenures as pastor of First Baptist Church, only one year, 1896–1897. His two most significant contributions to the church included strengthening Sunday school work and beginning a Women's Missionary Society. Prior to the associational meeting in October 1896, the Nacogdoches and Chireno congregations conducted Sunday School institutes. Shortly after the associational meeting, similar institutes were conducted in the Garrison and Antioch churches. As a result, when the Association met the following year, fifteen member churches reported having Sunday schools, an increase of eleven over the four reported the previous year. Harrell's wife, Josephine, took the lead in establishing a Women's Missionary Society at First Baptist during his pastorate. This organization later became the Women's Missionary Union, or WMU.

The last minister to pastor First Baptist during the nineteenth century was Albert Bell Vaughn. Although Vaughn was at the church only slightly longer than Harrell, he established the church's legal status under Texas law by securing a charter, dated November 5, 1899. The church trustees who signed this instrument included Dr. Joel H. Barham, E. M. Dotson, R. C. Monk, James M. Seale, and June C. Harris. Robert Lindsey, Charles Perkins, and J. M. Seale witnessed the signatures, and Thomas E. Baker notarized the document.

Vaughn received the first raise given to a pastor since Holt's tenure when his salary was increased from $800 to $1,200. The money did not come entirely from the congregation because at that time the Baptist General Convention of Texas subsidized salaries paid to the pastors of some churches. Nacogdoches and Wichita Falls, as well as a few other congregations, benefited from this practice. Members of churches that did not receive these subsidies resented the practice, evidenced by a resolution passed by the Mount Zion Association that stated: "[I]f such churches are not able to afford the luxury of a $1,200 preacher alone, we believe that they should be resigned to the words of truth coming from

Adoniram Judson Holt, considered the "father" of First Baptist Church, served as its pastor on two occasions. During his second pastorate, he was instrumental in securing the prohibition of the sale of alcoholic beverages in Nacogdoches. *Courtesy of Charles Bright.*

the mouth of a $500 preacher."[4] Since the specific salary of $1,200 was mentioned in the resolution and the Nacogdoches church was the only one in the Association receiving such a subsidy, it might be concluded that the resolution was aimed directly at First Baptist.

At the end of fourteen years of existence as a church, the congregation of First Baptist enjoyed a position far ahead of the other churches in the city and "had no rival."[5] Probably this referred to the number of members. The congregation had grown so that the original frame building no longer accommodated the attendance at services, so the church launched a building campaign. The church hired local architect Diedrich Rulfs to design a new facility and demolished the original frame building to make room for the new church. While construction proceeded, services were held in the Old Opera House on the northwest corner of Main and North Church streets, later the site of Stephen F. Austin State University's Cole Art Center.

Rulfs designed a Gothic-style building with some Victorian features, similar to the plan he developed fourteen years later for Zion Hill First Baptist Church, the city's leading black Baptist congregation. A. W. Birdwell recalled that the building "contained several good rooms, making a modern Sunday school possible."[6] Construction began during Vaughn's pastorate in the spring of 1899, and the building was completed at a cost of $13,000 early in the spring of 1900.

This downtown scene on the town square shows a crowd gathered to support the elimination of the sale of beverage alcohol in Nacogdoches. The pastor of First Baptist Church, A. J. Holt, and the Methodist minister were leaders of the successful prohibition forces. *First Baptist Church Archives.*

First Baptist Church held its first service in the new building on Sunday, April 1, 1900. The Reverend William Thomas Tardy, the congregation's new pastor, delivered the morning message. In his autobiography, Tardy recalled, "My inaugural as pastor was celebrated in the just-finished new church building."[7] Thus First Baptist began the twentieth century with both a new building and a new pastor.

At twenty-six, Tardy was among the youngest men to serve the church as pastor. He had already served as pastor of churches in Camden, Arkansas, as well as Longview, Palestine, Paris, and Greenville, Texas, and he had a reputation for being an excellent speaker with flawless English. Like Holt and Vaughn, Tardy served as trustee of the East Texas Baptist Institute at Rusk. He resigned in the fall of 1902, leaving the Sunday school and the other organizations of the church in "flourishing condition." He described his ministry in Nacogdoches as "not characterized by any outstanding features," but supported by "the strong men of the community."[8]

In the fall of 1901, the church called former pastor A. J. Holt, then serving as secretary of missions of the Tennessee Baptist Association, to deliver the dedicatory message for its new building. Holt had been a successful pastor of the church and was known affectionately as its "father," so the congregation turned to him when Tardy resigned. A strong advocate of missions, Holt began his second pastorate of First Baptist just as the denominational controversy over missionary endeavors again raised its head in the local association. The controversy had caused a split in the Baptist General Convention of Texas in 1901, resulting in the formation of a new organization, the Baptist Missionary Association of Texas. Holt managed to prevent a split in the Nacogdoches Baptist Association and kept it in the BGCT by securing the passage of an associational resolution that prevented the body from considering "any divisive measures touching the constitution."[9]

On May 6, 1903, Holt reported on the first six months of his second term as pastor in a letter mailed to each member of the congregation. He stated that during this brief period the church had experienced a net gain of 52 members for a total of 171, or more than half of the identified Baptists in Nacogdoches and the surrounding vicinity. He praised the members of the congregation and expressed appreciation for the church's organizations—the Sunday school, the Women's Missionary Society, the Ladies' Aid Society, the Baptist Young People's Union, and the Junior Union. After expressing his gratitude, Holt took the congregation to task, stating that only about 10 percent of the members attended prayer meeting regularly and half never attended; only about one-fifth attended business meetings, and two-thirds had not been to a business meeting for two

"HURRAH! HURRAH! FOR PROHIBITION SHOUT! HURRAH FOR THE NOBLE MEN WHO VOTE THE WHISKEY OUT!"

A. J. Holt Sung to the tune of "The Bonnie Blue Flag"

years. Of the 171 members, he said, only 25 attended Sunday services regularly, 107 attended occasionally, and 35 had not attended for at least a year. He observed that 95 of the 171 church members were women, but only 15 of them belonged to the Ladies' Aid Society, and the same fifteen constituted, for the most part, the Women's Missionary Society and the teachers in the Sunday school. Although fifty members had given a total of about $500 to missions, more than one hundred members had given nothing at all, and Holt enclosed a pledge card with his letter in their envelopes.

A man of strong convictions and never one to run from a fight on a matter of principle, Holt and W. W. Watts, the Methodist minister in Nacogdoches, joined forces in 1905 with the Women's Christian Temperance Union and the Anti-Saloon League to take on the city's saloonkeepers in a local option election to prohibit the sale of alcoholic beverages in the city. He and Watts campaigned hard, speaking in every community in the county, both white and black. Holt even composed a campaign song sung to the old Confederate tune, "Bonnie Blue Flag." Holt spoke so vigorously during the campaign that, for a time, he lost his voice. In his later years, he recalled how the pro-alcohol faction schemed to prevent the election results from being announced. They secured an injunction from a sympathetic district judge in Houston to prevent county officials from declaring and recording the results of the election and the local newspaper from publishing them. Unknown to them, however, the dry forces had planted an observer in the group that went to Houston to seek the injunction. This observer wired the information to the leaders of the dry faction in Nacogdoches, and before the delegation returned with the injunction, the prohibition forces leased the local newspaper for two weeks and sent the county clerk on a fishing trip. The county judge, who was sympathetic to the prohibitionists, wrote out the election results and immediately left for the St. Louis World's Fair. With no elected officials available to serve the injunction, the election results stood, and Nacogdoches County remained dry until 1971 when off-premises

Robert Monk, one of the early leaders of First Baptist Church, taught the Young Men's Sunday School Class for many years. When the class grew too large for its quarters in the church, it met in downtown movie theatres until the completion of the church's Education Annex in 1934. The class became known as the R. C. Monk Class after Dr. A. W. Birdwell became its teacher. This photograph was taken sometime between 1932 and 1942. *First Baptist Church Archives.*

consumption of alcoholic beverages was approved by a narrow margin of ninety-seven votes. Those opposed to the sale of alcoholic beverages later made another attempt to prohibit the sale of alcohol in Nacogdoches but were not successful. After the election, Holt and Watts were each presented gold-headed walking sticks to commemorate their part in the prohibition victory.

Throughout his second pastorate of the Nacogdoches church, Holt continued to play an active role in denominational affairs, serving as a director of the Baptist General Convention of Texas, trustee of the East Texas Baptist Institute at Rusk, and as a delegate to the meetings of the state convention.

While his voice was still recovering from the strain of campaigning in the local option election, Holt resigned to accept the presidency of Tennessee Baptist College in Knoxville, Tennessee. He noted in his autobiography that "the entire congregation was in tears" at the farewell service for him.[10] Both the Methodist and Presbyterian ministers testified that he had been a blessing to each of them. During his first Nacogdoches pastorate, Holt had been responsible for the Presbyterian minister's conversion, and the Methodist minister received his theological training in the Bible Institute Holt organized.

Mrs. Robert Lindsey (shown on the back row at left by the porch column) taught the Young Women's Sunday School Class. Other members of the class are Ellisee Harris Davidson (back row), Sallie T. Summers (middle row), Avie Stroud (middle row), Mattie Sanders Perry (middle row), Jennie June Harris (front row), and Emma Summers Mast (front row). *First Baptist Church Archives.*

The decade following Holt's second pastorate at First Baptist, like the decade following his first pastorate, resulted in a series of brief pastoral tenures of only one or two years each. The first to follow Holt was Aaron John Miller, the eighth man to serve the congregation as pastor in twenty-one years. A native of Mississippi, Miller, like those who preceded him as pastor of the church, was active in both local and state denominational affairs. He, too, served as trustee of the East Texas Baptist Institute and in 1906 led the Nacogdoches Baptist Association to encourage the organization of women's work in the association's churches. Miller's brief, two-year pastorate saw the church's Sunday school grow from nine teachers and 125 pupils in 1905 to twelve teachers and 150 pupils in 1906. The church's membership grew from 256 in 1906 to 276 in 1907, when Miller resigned to accept the call of the First Baptist Church of Leland, Mississippi.

Roe Thomas Holleman, a native East Texan from Rusk, followed Miller. At only twenty-two years old, he was the youngest pastor to serve First Baptist, and his tenure was also one of the shortest. After only a year, Holleman left Nacogdoches to attend Baylor University in Waco. Sadly, First Baptist would be his last pastorate; Holleman died in 1912 while still pursuing his studies at Baylor.

First Baptist's next pastor, Joseph Warren Bates, was a New Yorker who attended Southern Baptist Theological Seminary in Louisville, Kentucky. When called by the Nacogdoches congregation, Bates served as pastor of the First Baptist Church of Mexia. It is uncertain just when he arrived in Nacogdoches, but it had to be sometime in 1908 or early 1909 since the church's associational letter for 1909 listed him as pastor. During his brief tenure, the church hosted a two-week revival in January 1910, featuring William Walker, a noted Baptist evangelist of the time. The meeting resulted in ninety conversions, including a number of individuals such as James (Jim) R. Summers and Fannie Campbell Buchanan, who became longtime members of the congregation. Bates was remembered as a strong pre-millinnealist who loved horses and bore a slight resemblance to Theodore Roosevelt. He left Nacogdoches to serve in Big Spring, Texas.

Thomas Coleman Mahan began his service to the church in January 1911, succeeding Bates. During Mahan's tenure, the pastor's salary was increased from $1,350 to $1,800. The Mahan family probably welcomed this increase, since he and his wife were the parents of ten children. Like other pastors before him, Mahan served as trustee of the Rusk Baptist Institute. He left Nacogdoches after three years to accept the call of the First Baptist Church of Huntsville, Texas.

During Mahan's tenure a Young Men's Class that later became the R. C. Monk Sunday School Class was organized. The class had its beginnings in 1912 with R. C. Monk as its teacher and Robert Lindsey as secretary and song leader. Mrs. Lindsey taught the Young Women's Class, organized about this same time. The classes met in two small rooms at the rear of the church building Diedrich Rulfs designed, and attendance was stimulated by a friendly rivalry between the classes. The men's class outgrew its meeting place and moved to the Palace Theatre, where it continued to draw large numbers of men of all denominations. Mrs. Robert Lindsey played the piano, and her husband led the singing. On Sunday mornings members visited the downtown hotels and invited the men they found there, as well as those on the streets, to attend the class. Attendance frequently reached 100–150 men, and on special occasions the theatre was sometimes filled to capacity. In 1923 the class moved to the new Texan Theatre on Main Street and continued to meet there until completion of the church's Education Annex in 1934. When Monk became ill in 1923, Dr. A. W. Birdwell, the president of Stephen F. Austin State Teachers College, just getting underway in Nacogdoches, became the teacher. The name of the class was changed to the R. C. Monk Class in honor of its first teacher. It continued for many years, its members remaining young in spirit, if not in age.

The next pastor to serve First Baptist was a native of Missouri, Cornelius Albert Westbrook, who came to Nacogdoches early in the fall of 1914 from the First Baptist Church of Minden, Louisiana. Westbrook served the church for almost six years, ending the pattern of one- and two-year pastorates that had developed after Holt's second tenure at

Mrs. Robert Lindsey, for many years the organist at First Baptist Church, also taught Sunday school and a children's music class. This picture of her music class was taken about 1910 on the front steps of the Gothic-style church building designed for First Baptist by Diedrich Rulfs. *First Baptist Church Archives.*

First Baptist. As a young man, Westbrook left school to work as a farm laborer and later in a mercantile company in his hometown of Ashland, Missouri. While working at the mercantile company, he felt the call to preach and was tutored by the local school superintendent so he could enter college and prepare for the ministry. While still in college, he served as a part-time pastor. Later he recalled his first baptismal experience.

During the early part of the twentieth century, the Palacios Baptist Encampment was a popular spiritual retreat for members of First Baptist Church. This picture of First Baptist members at the encampment was taken about 1910. *First Baptist Church Archives.*

A four-week revival resulted in sixty-five candidates for baptism. It took Westbrook one and a half hours to immerse all sixty-five, but he stated that he did so "with no incident to mar the occasion."[11] At the time of his arrival, First Baptist reported a membership of 263, but within a year the membership had grown to 361.

Westbrook secured the services of outstanding Baptist preachers to hold annual revivals each spring, among them Dr. L. R. Scarborough, president of Southwestern Baptist Theological Seminary, in 1915; Dr. H. L. Winburn, pastor of Walnut Street Baptist Church in Louisville, Kentucky, in 1916; and Dr. George W. Truett, pastor of First Baptist Church in Dallas, Texas, in 1917. Westbrook himself remained a popular revival preacher with nearby Baptist congregations, such as those at Melrose and Lilly Grove.

During Westbrook's time at First Baptist, the United States entered World War I, and he led the congregation in devoting both Sunday services on July 22, 1917, to say farewell to local men leaving for military service and pray for their safe return. Two years later, as the war drew to a close, Westbrook resigned to accept the pastorate of the First Baptist Church of Warrensburg, Missouri. He later served in Missouri as the state secretary of missions and pastor of several other Missouri congregations, as well as the First Baptist Church of Charleston, South Carolina. In 1959, when Westbrook, at the age of eighty-seven, returned to Nacogdoches to participate in the church's seventy-fifth anniversary celebration, he still played eighteen holes of golf and performed pastoral supply work.

In March 1920, Samuel David Dollahite, a native of Hallsville, Texas, then serving as pastor of the First Baptist Church of Kaufman, Texas, accepted the call of First Baptist to become its thirteenth pastor. He served as pastor when the Texas legislature passed a bill authorizing Stephen F. Austin State Teachers Normal College in 1921 and preparations began for opening the new college in Nacogdoches. During his tenure the church had an active Sunday school, Baptist Young People's Union, and Women's Missionary Society. Like pastors before him, Dollahite took an active part in denominational affairs, serving as trustee of the Rusk Baptist Institute and on the executive board of the Baptist General Convention of Texas. He began collecting a "White Christmas Offering" to support the work of Buckner Orphan's Home in Dallas, Texas. This offering became a First Baptist tradition that continued for many years.

In December 1922, Dollahite resigned to accept a call from the First Baptist Church of Marlin, Texas. In evidence of the high esteem the congregation had for him, J. H. Summers moved that the church not accept his resignation. The motion failed only after Dollahite asked the membership to accept the resignation since he had made his decision with "much thought and prayer."[12] Also evident of the esteem of the church for him was the fact that he had received the highest salary the church had ever paid to a pastor until that time. His salary in 1920, $2,400, represented 64 percent of the total church budget, and he received raises to $2,850 and $3,000 in 1921 and 1922, respectively.

As Dollahite left Nacogdoches to report to his new congregation in Marlin, officials prepared to open the new state teachers college in Nacogdoches. The college president, Dr. A. W. Birdwell, and several other early members of the college faculty and administration placed their membership in First Baptist and were active in promoting the college ministry. As it anticipated the first influx of students, the congregation began to plan seriously for their arrival.

Dr. Allen Reed stands behind the original pulpit from the second building occupied by First Baptist Church. Its style matches the Gothic architecture of the church designed by Diedrich Rulfs. It was placed in the lower auditorium of the new brick building constructed in 1942. Twice rescued from fires, the pulpit is used weekly by the Senior Adult Sunday School Department. *Photo by Jonathan Canfield.*

1. A. J. Holt, *Pioneering in the Southwest* (Nashville, TN: The Sunday School Board of the Southern Baptist Convention, 1923), p. 234.

2. Ibid., p. 234.

3. Ibid., p. 235.

4. W. T. Parmer, *Seventy-five Years in Nacogdoches: A History of the First Baptist Church, 1884–1959* (Dallas, TX: Dorsey Co., 1959), p. 74.

5. Ibid., p. 75.

6. A. W. Birdwell, "First Baptist Church of Nacogdoches" (MS in First Baptist Church Archives, 1945), p. 11.

7. Parmer, *op. cit.*, p. 76.

8. Ibid., p. 76.

9. Holt, *op. cit.*, pp. 265–266.

10. Ibid., p. 270.

11. Parmer, *op. cit.*, p. 216.

12. Ibid., p. 94.

3

A Future Full of Promise

"The future is, I think, full of promise."

Dr. A. W. Birdwell
Minutes of the Board of Regents, 1925–1926
Stephen F. Austin State Teachers College

THE REVEREND BONNIE GRIMES SERVED AS PASTOR OF FIRST BAPTIST Church for sixteen years, the second-longest tenure in the church's history. His pastorate spanned the years of 1923 to 1939, a time when the opening of Stephen F. Austin State Normal College held much promise for both Nacogdoches and First Baptist Church. Grimes arrived in Nacogdoches in the spring of 1923, only a few months before the college opened, and his pastorate was marked by intense efforts to minister to the students enrolled in the new college. In the Sunday evening service on October 21, 1923, Joseph P. Boone, secretary of the Students' Department of the Baptist General Convention of Texas, spoke to the congregation about the need for a student ministry at the new college. The close association of First Baptist Church with Stephen F. Austin and of the congregation's ongoing concern for ministering to college students began with this event. The school's president, Dr. A.W. Birdwell, joined the church prior to the college's opening. His leadership and that of other early members of the

Opposite: The Reverend Bonnie Grimes served the second-longest tenure as pastor of First Baptist Church. He came to the church in 1923 and served the congregation for sixteen years. Among Grimes' most significant accomplishments were placing the church on a sound financial footing, establishing the mission that became Fredonia Hill Baptist Church, constructing the three-story brick Educational Annex, and setting the precedent of strong support for ministry to students enrolled at Stephen F. Austin State University. *First Baptist Church Archives.*

Stephen F. Austin faculty and administration who became active members of First Baptist Church, such as the college auditor, J. H. Wiseley, and C. H. Osborne, undoubtedly helped to focus the congregation's attention on ministering to this new segment of the town's population. Birdwell later recalled, "The work of the church among the students of Stephen F. Austin College will be remembered by this writer with deep gratitude as long as he shall live. Students have been converted and their faith strengthened. Many of them today are leaders in right thinking and worthy living [as a result of the work of First Baptist Church]."[1]

Grimes went to work quickly after he arrived in Nacogdoches. By the end of October 1923, he had conducted three revival meetings in the city, one in the Fredonia Hill neighborhood, another in the Frost-Johnson Mill area, and still another at West End Tabernacle. The meetings on Fredonia Hill resulted in the establishment of the first of six mission churches that were started and supported by First Baptist.

Prior to Grimes' revival in the Fredonia Hill neighborhood, Miss Sallie T. Summers and other members of the First Baptist Women's Missionary Society conducted Bible studies in homes in the southern part of town. The participants in these Bible studies, along with the new converts baptized by Grimes, formed the nucleus of the Fredonia Hill Mission sponsored by First Baptist. In 1923 the church purchased a site for the mission and erected a small, unpainted frame building with four walls and no windows. Members of the mission conducted their Sunday school classes in the building and then went to the First Baptist auditorium on North Street for worship services and Wednesday night prayer meetings. On Sunday afternoons and sometimes on Friday nights, Grimes preached at the mission. By 1934, the congregation had grown to about twenty-five members and was strong enough to become an independent church with the Reverend K. A. Woods as pastor. Since that time Fredonia Hill Baptist Church has been one of the major Baptist congregations in the city. Another church,

The first president of Stephen F. Austin State Normal College was Dr. A. W. Birdwell. Soon after arriving in Nacogdoches in 1922, Dr. Birdwell placed his membership in First Baptist. Dr. Birdwell assumed a leadership role in church affairs, serving as deacon, Sunday school teacher, and chairman of numerous committees. He remained a faithful member of the congregation until his death in 1954. *First Baptist Church Archives.*

Hoya Hill Baptist Church, located in the Frost-Johnson Mill area, also resulted from a revival conducted by Grimes, but it was not sponsored by First Baptist Church.

The second mission church sponsored by First Baptist was located in the Spanish-speaking Bonaldo community about ten miles west of town. Like the Fredonia Hill mission, the Bonaldo mission was preceded by several years of work conducted by the First Baptist Women's Missionary Society led by Miss Sallie T. Summers, Mrs. W. U. Perkins, Mrs. D. W. Buchanan, and Mrs. H. R. Mast. The Bible studies these ladies conducted met at various times on logs beside the road, in homes, and in an abandoned schoolhouse. In 1934, Grimes invited Dr. Paul Bell to bring four young Hispanic preachers from Bastrop to hold a two-week revival meeting at Bonaldo. The converts from this meeting were baptized in the Angelina River and were part of the initial membership of the mission congregation. Benito Villareal, a graduate of the Bell School in Bastrop, served as the mission's first pastor, and was supported financially by First Baptist and the Baptist State Mission Board. For a while Villareal conducted services on benches under trees on

The Reverend Bonnie Grimes was pastor of First Baptist when Stephen F. Austin State Normal College was established in Nacogdoches. Grimes quickly saw the potential for ministry and led the congregation to reach out to the college students. In this photograph taken in 1929, the First Baptist College Sunday School Class is shown on the steps of the Gothic-style church designed by Diedrich Rulfs. Grimes and Dr. C. H. Osborne are at the left rear of the top row. Mrs. Grimes and Mrs. Osborne are standing next to them. *First Baptist Church Archives.*

In 1923, First Baptist established Fredonia Hill Mission, the first of six mission churches sponsored by the congregation. Located in the southern part of Nacogdoches, its charter membership was composed of participants in neighborhood Bible studies led by the women of First Baptist and converts from a revival held in the area by the Reverend Grimes. *Photo by Tom Atchison.*

the property of a Catholic friend, Lucas Ynfantes. After more than a year of meeting outside in all kinds of weather, First Baptist provided the congregation with a building on two acres in the Bonaldo community. The Bonaldo Mission Chapel was dedicated on Sunday, June 16, 1935. The mission was slow to grow, partly due to the fact that the Spanish-speaking population of the area was mostly Catholic. It had grown to only sixty-four members when it became an independent church in 1948. By the fall of 1966, the congregation ceased to operate as a church, and First Baptist sold the building and land.

During Grimes' pastorate, First Baptist experienced a rapid increase in membership partially due to the influx of students enrolled in the college and the congregation's efforts to minister to them. During his first year, membership in the Sunday school grew from 364 to 555. There was also an increase in the Baptist Young People's Union and the beginning of a Baptist Layman's Union, an early forerunner of the Brotherhood organization and of the First Baptist Church Men's Ministry.

Throughout his Nacogdoches pastorate, Grimes served in leadership roles in Baptist work. He was the associational moderator of the Nacogdoches Baptist Association and its successor, the Shelby-'Doches Baptist Association. He was also active in other denominational work, including serving on the executive board of the Baptist General Convention of Texas and as a trustee for Marshall College, later East Texas Baptist University.

Bonaldo Mission, located in a Spanish-speaking community west of Nacogdoches, was the second mission church sponsored by First Baptist. Prior to the establishment of the mission church, the First Baptist Women's Missionary Society held Bible studies in the community. Three of the Bible study leaders are shown in the foreground of this picture. From left to right, they are Mrs. Fannie Buchanan, Mrs. Will Perkins, and Miss Sallie T. Summers. At the far left rear are Jimmie Jones and George Middlebrook (in hat). The mission church building is in the background. *First Baptist Church Archives.*

By 1935, the Southern Baptist Convention was encouraging tithing as a means of supporting the work of the denomination and of the local churches. Grimes quickly seized the opportunity to encourage his local congregation to become tithers. In June of that year, the *Daily Sentinel* reported that the church had voted to encourage its members to commit to tithing for a three-month trial basis. By fall the church adopted a system of financing church operations based on a budget underwritten by pledged contributions of the membership. On Sunday, November 17, Grimes preached a special message on the necessity of supporting the church financially and passed out cards for members to use to make their pledges in support of the church's budget. Two days later a banquet, sponsored by the R. C. Monk Sunday School Class and served by the ladies of the church, was held to promote underwriting the budget. This was the beginning of using a systematic method of church finance at First Baptist that replaced the old method in which the church treasurer went around to the members and collected money to pay the pastor's weekly salary whenever Sunday collections were not sufficient to do so.

Converts from the Bonaldo Mission are shown being baptized by mission pastor, the Reverend Roy Monzingo, in the Angelina River. Monzingo is to the right with his hand raised. *First Baptist Church Archives.*

Soon after the opening of SFA in the fall of 1923, discussions regarding "a new meeting house" for the church began. In 1928–1929 plans for a completely new church estimated to cost $150,000 were made. Efforts at raising the funds required resulted in $38,000 in pledges, most to be paid "when and if a contract should be let." The Great Depression intervened, and the building project was put on hold. Some church members, especially women, contributed to a building fund on a regular basis, and by 1932, the fund had grown to $14,000. Because of the financial conditions of the times, the deacons decided to construct a three-story brick educational an-

nex in the rear of the wooden structure designed by Diedrich Rulfs rather than undertake the entire project. Dr. A. W. Birdwell chaired the building committee composed of J. H. Wiseley, R. C. Monk, and J. E. Reese. John Hamblin, a local contractor, was paid a monthly salary by the church to employ workmen and supervise the construction, while Robert Lindsey, a longtime church member, assisted in purchasing the building materials. The annex cost $18,000 and was entirely paid for upon completion. It contained twenty-eight classrooms, two assembly rooms, office space, and other ancillary rooms. Birdwell recalled that the completion of this annex made it possible for the church to have a modern Sunday school and

In 1932, First Baptist constructed a three-story brick Educational Annex in the rear of the wooden Gothic-style church designed by Diedrich Rulfs. This building was incorporated into later construction projects of the congregation and continues as an integral part of the church's facilities. This picture is a view of the rear of the building looking east toward North Street. *First Baptist Church Archives.*

In 1948, members of First Baptist worked with other Baptist congregations in the city and with the Baptist General Convention of Texas Executive Board to establish a Baptist Bible Chair at Stephen F. Austin State Teachers College. A two-story frame building located on East College Street adjacent to the campus served as the Baptist Student Center and home for the Bible teacher and his family. *First Baptist Church Archives.*

better provide for the needs of the young people of the congregation. This concern for providing appropriate space for Christian education and to minister to the needs of children and youth continued to be a major impetus in future building projects undertaken by the church.

In the spring of 1939, Grimes resigned the pastorate of First Baptist to accept the call of the First Baptist Church of Bastrop, where he served until his death on Sunday, April 25, 1943. During his tenure at the Nacogdoches church, the congregation experienced unprecedented growth in membership, constructed additional facilities, and significantly expanded church programs, including beginning the student work at SFA. Grimes was recalled fondly by the members of the congregation as a "genial" individual who liked fishing and pie, frequently saying to the ladies who served at church dinners, "I love only two kinds of pie—hot pie and cold pie."[2]

Following Grimes' resignation, the church called a student enrolled in the Southern Baptist Theological Seminary in Louisville, Kentucky, to serve as interim pastor. Answering this call began a lifelong association with First Baptist for Harold Lord Fickett Jr. During his service as interim in the summer of 1939, Fickett met Mary Frances Dorsey, the daughter of longtime First Baptist members James and Lorene Dorsey and a senior at Stephen F. Austin State College. Their romance blossomed, and the following June they were married in the last wedding held in the wooden church building designed by Diedrich Rulfs. Fickett later had a distinguished career as a Baptist minister, serving at Tremont Temple in Boston, Massachusetts; First Baptist Church of Van Nuys, California; and Faith Evangelical Church in Chatsworth, California.

The Reverend William B. Coble, a graduate of Howard Payne College and Southwestern Baptist Theological Seminary, was the first full-time director of the Stephen F. Austin Baptist Student Union. Coble's brother, Charles, met and married Joy Prince, the daughter of longtime First Baptist members Ezra and Iva Prince, while he was attending Stephen F. Austin. *First Baptist Church Archives.*

Regardless of where he served, the Fickett family always considered Nacogdoches home, returning frequently to hold revivals and conduct Bible studies for local congregations. When he retired from the ministry, Fickett and his wife returned to Nacogdoches and became members of First Baptist once again.

Jared I. Cartlidge succeeded Grimes as pastor of First Baptist Church. He was the only native of Nacogdoches to pastor the church and one of only two ministers to pastor the congregation twice. His father, B. R. Cartlidge, was a Baptist minister who was ordained by the church and served several congregations in Nacogdoches County in the early years of the twentieth century before moving his family to Athens, where young Jared grew up and was graduated from high school.

Cartlidge's first pastorate began in the fall of 1939, when he resigned the First Baptist Church of Eastland to accept the call to fill the pulpit in Nacogdoches left vacant by Grimes' resignation. His ministry at First Baptist was characterized by continuation of the growth begun under Grimes' ministry, eliminating the debt on the parsonage, and construction of a new auditorium building. Within a year of his arrival, the average Sunday school attendance grew from 286 to 314. Training Union attendance made similar gains, growing his first year from an average of 103 on Sunday evenings to an average of 150.

Cartlidge quickly led the church to pay off its indebtedness of $3,976 on the parsonage and revived plans for a new auditorium put on hold during the Depression. In July 1940, a building committee and a building finance committee were appointed. Separate committees were appointed to make recommendations for purchasing and financing an electric organ for the new auditorium.

In only ten months, the building finance committee reached its goal of $12,000 in cash, and it set a second goal of $10,000 in pledges that was

Robert Lindsey, a Nacogdoches businessman, worked in numerous leadership roles at First Baptist during the first half of the twentieth century. He was instrumental in securing building materials for construction of the brick Educational Annex in 1934. His wife served as organist for the church for many years. *First Baptist Church Archives.*

During the summer of 1939, Dr. Harold L. Fickett Jr. served as interim pastor of First Baptist between the service of the Reverend Bonnie Grimes and the first pastorate of Dr. Jared I. Cartlidge. It was then that Fickett met his future wife, Mary Frances Dorsey, daughter of First Baptist members James and Lorene Dorsey. Shown here are the members of the Fickett family in the 1950s. Seated in front are Dr. Fickett and Mary Frances with Harold between them. Standing behind their parents are Mary and Ruth. *First Baptist Church Archives.*

exceeded in less than eight months. The cash and pledges, a loan of $30,000 from the M. A. Anderson Foundation in Houston, Texas, and interim financing provided by the Commercial National Bank of Nacogdoches enabled the church to begin construction.

The congregation employed local architect Hal Tucker to design its new building. Tucker presented plans for a Colonial-style building of red brick trimmed in white stone with fluted white columns. The building included a new auditorium with a balcony, a basement with a kitchen, an elevated baptistery behind the pulpit, and a pastor's study. The design of the facility allowed it to occupy the same space as the existing wooden auditorium located in front of the Educational Annex. Its rear wall joined the annex, so it was necessary to demolish the old wooden building before construction could begin.

On October 2, 1941, demolition of the wood-frame building designed by Diedrich Rulfs began, and six days later construction started on the new facility. John Hamblin, who successfully supervised the construction of the Educational Annex in 1932, was hired to oversee construction of this project. A tabernacle erected at the rear of the Educational Annex housed worship services during the construction of the new auditorium.

This was the first of two times that the congregation worshiped in a temporary tabernacle on the church grounds, both occurring when Cartlidge served the church as pastor.

Construction on the new church plant was underway when the United States entered World War II in December 1941. In spite of the shortages caused by the nation's mobilization for war, the new church building was finished by the summer of 1942. On Sunday, July 19, only a little more than a year after the building committee had been appointed, the first services were held in the new auditorium. In the afternoon, Mrs. Harry McLain of Houston played a concert on the new electric organ, and in the evening worship service, Cartlidge baptized candidates in the new, elevated baptistery behind the pulpit. No longer was it necessary for the men of the church to move the pulpit and remove the floorboards of the platform to access the baptistery, as they had to do in the old church.

With additional classroom space for adults available in the new building, Cartlidge attempted to organize the Sunday school classes into age groups in accordance with Baptist denominational recommendations. Then, as now, many adults were less than enthusiastic about changing classes just to be with their appropriate age group. One church member, Mrs. Robert Lindsey, stated in her diary that "Sunday School in basement of new church first time [*sic*]. Much reorganizing—trying to get various 'generations' classed—I am supposed to be among the *100 year olds*, but 'I bucked' and *so did Rob*."[3] Such efforts to grade the adult Sunday School classes continued for another half century before the church's ministerial staff recognized the futility of dictating to adults which class they should attend.

Dr. Jared I. Cartlidge was the only native of Nacogdoches to serve First Baptist as pastor, and he did so on two occasions, 1939–1942 and 1951–1954. *First Baptist Church Archives.*

The original parsonage of First Baptist Church was a single-story, bungalow-style house located on the northwestern corner of North Street and Muller Street. First Baptist pastors and their families occupied this home until a new parsonage on Garner Street was purchased in 1955. Dr. Bill Crook and his wife Eleanor were the last to occupy this parsonage. *First Baptist Church Archives.*

Lottie Moon Bible

Miss Blanche Rose Walker, a Southern Baptist missionary to China for thirty-two years, was supported in her work by First Baptist Church. Before her death she gave this Bible to Miss Sallie T. Summers, a longtime member of the church. "Miss Sallie T" later donated the Bible to the church, stating that it was once used by the famous Southern Baptist missionary to China, Lottie Moon, and given by her to Miss Walker. This copy of the Bible serves as a reminder of the congregation's long history of support for missions. On numerous occasions the church has used the Bible to promote the Southern Baptist Convention's annual Christmas offering for international missions named in honor of Miss Moon.

Oral tradition attributes this Bible to the great Southern Baptist Missionary to China, Lottie Moon. *Photo by Jonathan Canfield.*

Miss Walker served as a Baptist missionary to China from 1905 to 1937. The First Baptist Women's Missionary Society helped support her work in China and she visited the congregation when home on furlough. She was a contemporary of Lottie Moon, and the "Lottie Moon Bible" owned by First Baptist was given to her by Miss Moon in China. *First Baptist Church Archives.*

Almost immediately following the completion of the church's new facilities, Cartlidge resigned to accept the call of the First Baptist Church of Corsicana, Texas. His last Sunday to preach at First Baptist was September 20, 1942. For the next eight months, Dr. H. D. Bruce, president of East Texas Baptist College in Marshall, served the congregation as interim pastor. By the first Sunday in June 1943, the church had a new pastor, Lifus Earl Lamb.

The Reverend L. E. Lamb, a native of Missouri, came to Nacogdoches from the First Baptist Church of Mount Pleasant, Texas. His first sermon as pastor was delivered in the morning worship service on June 6, 1943. Lamb was recognized as an able preacher and pastor, but never a "seeker of popularity."[4] It was said that his congregations always knew where he stood on issues, and whenever there was a problem, he faced it head on. Perhaps this was a result of his military service in Europe in World War I. W. T. Parmer, in his biographical sketch of Lamb published in *Seventy-five Years in Nacogdoches*, related that there was controversy one Sunday morning over the annual promotion in the Sunday school. Lamb remarked, "Well, we have had some problems to face this morning, but we just took the bull by the horns and went ahead."[5] Lamb also was outspoken in his opposition to all forms of gambling in the

In 1942, First Baptist constructed a new Colonial-style brick building to replace the wooden church occupied by the congregation since 1900. Originally contemplated by the church early in 1929, construction of the new facility was delayed by the Great Depression. It was designed by Nacogdoches architect Hal Tucker. John Hamblin supervised construction of the building. *First Baptist Church Archives.*

The sanctuary of the building constructed in 1942 contained a raised platform and choir loft. To the rear of the choir loft and in the center of the platform was the baptistry covered by crimson drapery. The electric organ was centered on the platform at the front of the choir loft. The original windows contained amber glass that some said "cast a golden glow" over services. Shown in this picture of the interior is the wedding ceremony of longtime First Baptist members Mildred Grimes and Lester B. Sitton. *First Baptist Church Archives.*

community, from flipping coins to see who would pay for coffee to illegal slot machines. This tendency to approach matters head on was evident early in his ministry when, prior to accepting the church's call, he required a meeting with the deacons to make certain that they understood that his plans for the church included building a Sunday school that met the standards of the Southern Baptist Convention and strongly emphasizing tithing and stewardship.

Lamb's policies were successful, and there was significant progress in all areas of the church program during his tenure as pastor. By the end of Lamb's eight years as pastor, the average attendance of 579 in Sunday school exceeded its total enrollment when he arrived. The Training Union experienced similar growth, increasing from an enrollment of fewer than 100 at the beginning of his pastorate to an enrollment of 467 and an average attendance of 260 by the time he left. In addition to increasing the enrollment and attendance for the Sunday school and Training Union programs, in the fall of 1944, Lamb led the

In 1945, under the leadership of L. E. Lamb, First Baptist purchased the adjacent house and lot to the north of the church known as the Hardeman property. *First Baptist Church Archives.*

In 1946, only one year after purchasing the house and lot on its north side, First Baptist purchased the Matthews property on its south side from Cason, Monk & Company Funeral Home. Both houses provided educational space for the growing church. The corner of the Educational Annex and the 1942 sanctuary may be seen in the right background of this picture. Claudette (Fore) Sutton, whose father, Claude Fore, was the funeral director for Cason, Monk & Company for many years, recalls that her family lived in the upper stories of the house during her early years. *First Baptist Church Archives.*

men of the church in organizing a Baptist Brotherhood with an initial membership of thirty-two men with Pat Jackson as president. Vacation Bible schools during Lamb's pastorate were well attended, and growth was also experienced in the Royal Ambassador and Girl's Auxiliary programs.

Throughout his time at First Baptist, Lamb maintained a strong emphasis on presenting the gospel. Many well-known Baptist ministers and evangelists conducted revival services each year during his pastorate, and Lamb himself was often invited to preach revivals in other churches. Mrs. Lamb remembered that he always placed a strong emphasis on sermon preparation and used a tape recorder provided to the church by Lacy Hunt to polish his messages.

An immediate concern upon the arrival of Lamb and his wife, Miriam, son, Robert Lee, and the family collie, Patsy, was the condition of the church parsonage. Although Cartlidge had succeeded in eliminating the debt on the parsonage, Mrs. Lamb recalled that it was not in good condition. The congregation wanted to renovate the building before the new pastor and his family moved in, so they rented another house for them while the parsonage was remodeled, including installation of a second bathroom. After the renovations were complete and the Lamb family was settled in the house, a reception was held February 3, 1944, for the congregation to view the improvements.

Lamb's involvement in improving the church facilities extended beyond the parsonage; he also led the congregation to purchase two pieces of property adjoining the church lot to provide for expansion. In July

"WE LIVED NEXT DOOR TO THE CHURCH IN THE MATTHEWS HOUSE, WHICH SERVED AS CASON MONK FUNERAL HOME. [IT WAS] WHERE THE CHAPEL IS LOCATED NOW. ALTHOUGH MY FAMILY WAS METHODIST, I REMEMBER USING THE CHURCH BASEMENT TO ROLLER SKATE WITH BAPTIST FRIENDS."

Claudette (Fore) Sutton

The Reverend L. E. Lamb became First Baptist's sixteenth and third-longest tenured pastor in 1943. During his pastorate Lamb placed strong emphasis on evangelism and outreach, resulting in significant growth in the congregation's membership. In addition he improved the church facilities and gave strong support to the college ministry. *First Baptist Church Archives.*

1945, the house and lot adjoining the church property on the north, known as the Hardeman property, was purchased with $2,000 from the general fund and $8,000 from a note executed with Commercial National Bank. A year later the house and lot adjoining the church on the south was purchased from Cason, Monk & Company for $20,000. Known as the Matthews property, the house was used at that time for Cason, Monk & Company's funeral home business. Both of these structures were used for educational space for the growing congregation for the next twenty years. The single-story house on the north housed the Intermediate Department, and the two-story frame house on the south hosted the Young People's Department and office space for the new Shelby-'Doches Baptist Associational missionary, P. F. Squyres. Additional facility improvements made under Lamb's leadership included the installation of air conditioning in the church and the construction of a cabin for use by the church at Pineywoods Baptist Encampment.

The loan on the new brick auditorium constructed during the Cartlidge years provided for a ten-year payout, but as a result of Lamb's emphasis on tithing and stewardship, it was paid off in three years. To celebrate that achievement and to dedicate the structure, a note-burning ceremony and dedication service was held on Sunday, October 14, 1945. Jared I. Cartlidge, the church's pastor when the building was constructed, returned to preach the dedicatory sermon. At a special afternoon service, Dr. A. W. Birdwell, longtime church member, Sunday school teacher, deacon, and president emeritus of Stephen F. Austin State Teacher's College, reviewed the church's history, and brief comments were made by a number of other longtime members, including former pastor T. C. Mahan.

For many years Baptist congregations in East Texas have utilized Pineywoods Baptist Encampment at Woodlake located near Corrigan, Texas, for retreats and summer youth camps. During his pastorate, L. E. Lamb led First Baptist to construct a cabin for use by the congregation, especially its youth. The cabin had a central entrance with the boys' dorm and bath on the right and the girls' dorm and bath on the left. In this picture Jerry Prince is shown standing in the foreground with the First Baptist cabin in the rear. *First Baptist Church Archives.*

Conducting Vacation Bible Schools has been an annual summer ministry of First Baptist for the children of the congregation and other children of the community. These pictures show participants in the Vacation Bible School in 1940 on the front steps of the wooden church building that served the congregation from 1900 until 1942. *First Baptist Church Archives.*

Lamb's success in increasing the giving of the congregation raised the curiosity of members of the local Methodist church. His son, Robert Lee Lamb, recalled, "One day a delegation of laymen from the Methodist Church came to Dad's study at the church and demanded to know how the Baptists were able to do so well financially. 'What is your secret?' they wanted to know. As Dad was about to tell them, they added, 'And don't tell us about tithing, either.' So Dad just laughed and said he had nothing to say 'because they had just killed the goose that laid the golden egg.'"[6]

Lamb had a lifelong interest in music and even studied gospel music at Southwestern Baptist Theological Seminary in Fort Worth, Texas. As a result, he led the congregation to purchase a Steinway grand piano in 1950 and to replace the electric Organtron with an Aeolian Skinner pipe organ. Unfortunately, his pastorate ended before the organ was installed. Lamb's son, Robert Lee, shared his father's love of music. He played trombone in the school band, sang in both the church and college choirs, and frequently sang solos.

In addition to the responsibility of maintaining her home, Mrs. Lamb supported and worked beside her husband, frequently accompanying him to visit prospects and sick and shut-in church members. She assumed a major leadership role in the church's Women's Missionary Union, a large organization with about sixty women regularly attending its mission studies, book reviews, luncheons, and teas. In addition she taught the college Sunday school class and held an annual Christmas party for college students in the parsonage.

In her memoirs, Mrs. Lamb recalled that her husband went coatless during the hot, humid East Texas summers but always wore a starched

"IT WAS THROUGH THE BSU ORGANIZATION IN FEBRUARY 1946 THAT I MET MY FUTURE HUSBAND, TRAVIS N. PRICE, WHO HAD JUST RETURNED FROM WORLD WAR II. MISS [SUE] BARKSDALE [FIRST BAPTIST CHURCH SECRETARY AND PART-TIME BSU DIRECTOR] WAS INSTRUMENTAL IN GETTING MANY OF THE VETERANS TO ATTEND FIRST BAPTIST. THE REVEREND L. E. LAMB MARRIED US IN FIRST BAPTIST. THE CHURCH HAD A LARGE MEMBERSHIP. BYPU WAS OUTSTANDING WITH MRS. NORMAN (NINA) HILL AS DIRECTOR. AT THAT TIME YOU DID NOT BELONG TO FIRST BAPTIST UNLESS YOU ATTENDED BYPU!"

Carolyn (Muckleroy) Price

L. D. Pate was a longtime member of First Baptist and partner in Mize Department Store. For many years he taught in the children's Sunday school departments. His nine-year-old boys' class in the 1940s contained three sets of twins—Billy and Bailey Nations, Joe and Gene Miller, and Leonard and Lonnie Case. *Courtesy of Anita Pate Standridge.*

white shirt and tie. Because she did not like to see him in a shirt that was limp and wrinkled, she made certain that there was a freshly ironed one for him to change into every day when he came home for lunch. In 1946, her parents' health began to fail, and she gave up teaching the college class and much of her other work in the church and moved her parents into the parsonage. Her father, Dr. F. M. McConnell, a much-respected and longtime editor of the state denominational newsletter, the *Baptist Standard*, died in 1947. Following her father's death, Mrs. Lamb continued to share the responsibility of caring for her mother with a sister. She also opened the parsonage to their daughter, Lenore, for the birth of their granddaughter, and to a son of friends in Mount Pleasant who attended Stephen F. Austin College.

The years following the end of World War II were a time of rapid growth for Stephen F. Austin State College, as many returning servicemen took advantage of the G.I. Bill to complete their education. From the beginning of the college, members of First Baptist had been concerned with ministering to the students, and during the early part of Lamb's pastorate, the church secretary, Sue Barksdale, traveled on the city bus between the church and the college campus to coordinate the work of the Baptist Student Union. About this time the Baptist General Convention of Texas increased its support of Bible chairs at state colleges, including paying the salary of a Bible teacher and providing Baptist Student Union centers near campuses. Early in 1948 Lamb seized the opportunity to work

First Baptist Church Intermediate Royal Ambassador Chapter—1946. First row, left to right: James Redfield, Kenneth Fulmer, George Grigsby, Max Grigsby, Roland Burrows, and Everett Dorian. Second row, left to right: Robert Lee Lamb (pastor's son), Roy Collins, Norman Hill (director), L. E. Lamb (pastor), Charles Ray Dorian, Adrian Ballard, and Charles Shadden. *First Baptist Church Archives.*

with the other Baptist churches in the city, college president Dr. Paul L. Boynton, and the Baptist State Executive Board to establish a center and Baptist Bible chair at Stephen F. Austin. In May, William B. Coble was recommended to Dr. Boynton as the first teacher for the Bible chair. By the beginning of the fall semester, Coble, a graduate of Howard Payne College and Southwestern Baptist Theological Seminary, and his wife, moved into a two-story frame house on East College Street located immediately west of the Methodist Wesley Foundation Student Center. The house had been secured with the assistance of First Baptist to serve as the Baptist Student Center and the home of the Bible teacher. The Cobles lived in the upstairs rooms while the lower rooms were used for Bible classes and for student recreation. By the next semester, the number of Bible courses taught by Coble doubled from two to four and enrollment in them grew to fifty-five.

Establishing a Baptist presence in neighborhoods of the city where there was none continued to be a concern of the congregation. Early in 1948, the deacons and the Brotherhood began planning to establish a mission church to be known as the West Side Mission on the Douglass

The youngest children in the Southern Baptist youth mission organization during the mid-twentieth century were called Sunbeams. Shown on the steps of the 1942 church building are, first row, left to right, Gail Sowell, Henry Seale, Jimmy Partin, Susie Seale, Martha McClintock, Sissy McClintock, and David McClintock. Second row, left to right: Valerie Braselton, Nan Kennedy, Ann Sowell, Rose Ann Jones, Dorothy Mason, Rider Johnson, and Ann Collins. Third row, left to right: Mrs. S. F. Dunn, Mrs. Folden, George Fitch, Herman Wells, Lonnie Collins, and James Fitch. *First Baptist Church Archives.*

Highway (Texas State Highway 21 West). A mission building committee chaired by L. E. Moser and a mission finance committee chaired by F. L. Harris were appointed. On August 2, the deacons approved plans for a thirty-by-forty-foot furnished building costing $5,000. J. W. Dunn was hired as pastor, and services were held in the new mission beginning in October. This was the third mission church established by First Baptist Church. Later, as an independent church, it became known as Memorial Baptist Church.

First Baptist Church Girls Auxiliary Coronation Service–1948. Seated on first row, left to right: Faye Alexander, Evelyn Austin, Sylvia Johnson, Claudia Jones, Valerie Braselton, Laura Lee Johnson, Betty Collins, Carolyn Harris. Second row, left to right: Charles Christopher (crown bearer), Sue Braselton, Ann Orton, Keith Biggs (crown bearer), and Earl Alexander. Back row, left to right: Mrs. Elton Alexander (sponsor), Jean Prince, Sue Turner, Nancy Ruth Burrows, Martha Gee, Kitty Folden, Beth Alexander, Shirley McGee, Carol Ann Crawford, and Annelle Turner. *First Baptist Church Archives.*

Like those pastors who preceded him, Lamb was active in Baptist denominational affairs. During his time at First Baptist, Lamb served as moderator of the Shelby-'Doches Baptist Association, as president of District Two of the Baptist General Convention of Texas, on the Executive Board of the Baptist General Convention of Texas, and as trustee of East Texas Baptist College. Lamb resigned as pastor of

First Baptist Church Royal Ambassadors–1948. Front row, left to right: Lonnie Collins, George Fitch, Barry Hensley, Vidal Jones Jr. (son of FBC music minister), Gaylord Armstrong, Jerry Moorer, John Pack Thompson. Second row, left to right: Wayne Baker, John Hardin Lester, Duke Braselton, James Fitch, Earl Glynn Alexander. Back row, left to right: Don Evans (leader) and Elton Alexander (leader). *First Baptist Church Archives.*

This photograph shows the Sunbeams and Girls Auxiliaries in front of the organ in the sanctuary of the church building constructed in 1942. Front row, left to right: Sue Braselton, Rose Mary Ard, Mary Lynn Moorer, Kay Kennedy, Bruce Simpson, David Jones, Sylvia Jones, and Ann Orton. Back row, left to right: Tommy Biggs, Charles Christopher, William Everett Simpson, Elizabeth Hindman, Glenda Tipton, Milton Moorer, Keith Biggs, Jerry Tipton, and Claudia Jones. *First Baptist Church Archives.*

First Baptist Church on Sunday, June 24, 1951. He concluded his Nacogdoches ministry by baptizing the children that were converted in the previous week's vacation Bible school. Lamb's eight-year tenure as pastor was the third-longest in the church's history. It was marked by significant growth in church membership and giving, improvement of the church facilities, the establishment of a third mission church, and the expansion of the student work at Stephen F. Austin. Many members and former members of the congregation remembered Lamb and his family with great fondness.

"I REMEMBER R.A.'S WITH FONDNESS. IT'S A GOOD PROGRAM FOR BOYS. MY BROTHER [GEORGE FITCH] AND I RODE TO R.A.'S WITH ELTON ALEXANDER [THE LEADER] IN HIS CANDY TRUCK."

James Fitch

1. A. W. Birdwell, "First Baptist Church of Nacogdoches" (MS in First Baptist Church Archives, 1945), p. 9.

2. W. T. Parmer, *Seventy-five Years in Nacogdoches: A History of the First Baptist Church, 1884–1959* (Dallas, TX: Dorsey Co., 1959), p. 224.

3. Ibid., p. 105.

4. Ibid., p. 238.

5. Ibid., p. 239.

6. Robert Lee Lamb, "FBC Celebration" (Email to Jean Rudisill, July 20, 2008. Copy in First Baptist Church Archives).

4

Saints in the Sawdust

"...a church in the sawdust."

W. T. Parmer
*Seventy-five Years in Nacogdoches: A History
of the First Baptist Church, 1884–1959*

In September 1951, Jared I. Cartlidge became the seventeenth pastor of First Baptist Church and the second minister to serve as its pastor on two separate occasions. Following his first pastorate, Cartlidge remained extremely popular with the congregation of First Baptist. The Cartlidge family had a special feeling for Nacogdoches as well. The Cartlidges' daughter, Jaramy (Mrs. James Karns), remembered that her father "loved Nacogdoches and felt rooted there… He and mother loved the church family and were loved in return."[1]

After Lamb's resignation on June 30, 1951, Cartlidge was invited to preach a revival at the church during the first week in August. During the course of the revival, the congregation began to discuss asking him to pastor the church a second time. On August 26 the church extended a call, and Cartlidge resigned from the Seventh and James Baptist Church in Waco to return to Nacogdoches. By September he was back in Nacogdoches and making plans with the church to expand its educational and music ministries. As a first step in this expansion, the church extended a call to William (Bill) H. Wheeless of Victoria, Texas, to serve as director of education and music.

Opposite: In 1951, Dr. Jared I. Cartlidge was called by First Baptist to serve as its pastor a second time. Shown here, from left to right, are Cartlidge's daughter, Jaramy, Dr. Cartlidge, and Mrs. Cartlidge. Their son, Bouldin, dressed in his cowboy outfit, is standing in front. *First Baptist Church Archives.*

Additional space was needed to accommodate the existing departments and classes as well as provide for future growth. Since 1945 the youth departments of the Sunday school and Training Union had been housed in the two frame houses on either side of the church. Except for the church auditorium, rehearsal space for the church adult and youth choirs was virtually nonexistent, and the congregation had grown to the point that the basement and kitchen no longer adequately accommodated church suppers and socials. In February 1952, the congregation decided to plan new educational facilities, and by May a new building fund was established with a goal of raising $50,000 by January 1, 1953.

Before the church could accumulate the $50,000 or even decide what it should be used to construct, a fire severely damaged the main church building. A church member, Robert N. (Nick) Nicholson, was shopping across North Street from the church about 6:00 p.m. on Friday, October 17, 1952, when he saw smoke coming from the roof of the church and called in the alarm. The fire was already well underway when it was detected. When the alarm sounded, Nacogdoches Fire Marshal Reggie Reagan could see the fire's smoke from his location at a store on South Street. The impact of the fire was significant, damaging the roof, the heating and air conditioning system, and the new Aeolian Skinner pipe organ. The Nacogdoches Fire Department recently had acquired a new ladder truck, and Cartlidge credited its use and the quick response of the firemen with preventing even more extensive damage.

This view shows the choir loft and baptistry prior to the fires that destroyed the sanctuary in 1952 and 1953. In the center behind the organ are Palmer O'Barr, the minister of music, and the church organist, Mrs. C. L. Steed. Children in the choir are, left to right, first row, Harold Pate, unknown, Jerry Prince, Jerry Tipton, unknown, unknown, Judy Spradley, Peggy Doss, Robeleen Stewart, and Carol Whitten. Second row, William Everett Simpson, Jack Hammett, Glenda Tipton, Gail Sowell, Rose Ann Jones, Valarie Braselton, Ann Sowell, Faye Rene Alexander, Shirley Whitton, Robbie Hensarling, Billie Jo Holt, Laura Lee Johnson, Robert Gray, Jimmy Partin, and Butch Looney. *Photo courtesy of Ann Sowell Nerren.*

The attention of the congregation immediately focused on repairing the damages, and a committee chaired by John C. Crawford was appointed to oversee the restoration. The church basement suffered only smoke and water damage, so it was cleaned up and services were held in it while the auditorium was repaired. Because it was much smaller than the main auditorium, Cartlidge had to conduct two services on Sunday mornings.

After the repairs to the church were completed, the congregation turned its attention to the possibility of constructing additional educational facilities. Before any concrete plans were made, a second fire destroyed the church, leaving only the four walls of the auditorium standing. About 10:40 on Wednesday night, July 1, 1953, C. J. McBroom Jr., an attendant at a service station located just north of the church, heard "thumping" noises coming from the church.[2] Because he could not leave the station unattended, he asked three high school boys who had stopped at the station for gas to investigate. As they rounded the rear of the church drive, they saw smoke coming from the attic of the educational building and proceeded without stopping to Central Fire Station to report the fire. The flames were so intense that church member Anita (Pate) Standridge remembers being able to see them from her neighbor's house on Cooper Street, and Miss Irene Clevenger, another church member, watched flames shoot through the roof of the educational building from her home at 515 North Street. The first trucks arrived at the church about 10:45 p.m., but the fire was already out of control, and shortly after midnight the roof of the auditorium collapsed.

The next morning members of the congregation viewed the still smoldering ruins and attempted to salvage what items they could. Bill

"I WAS WATCHING THE FIRE FROM THE GULF SERVICE STATION NEXT DOOR WHEN THE FIRE CHIEF, DELBERT TEUTSCH, DROVE UP AND SHOUTED, "DON'T OPEN THE FRONT DOOR!" IT WAS TOO LATE. THE DOOR WAS BROKEN DOWN WITH AN AXE, AND A SMALL FIRE ERUPTED INTO A FIREBALL, DEMOLISHING EVERYTHING."

James Fitch

Although damage from the first fire was mostly from smoke and water, the second fire on July 1, 1953, completely gutted the interior of the sanctuary. The twisted, charred steel beams that supported the roof were all that remained in the auditorium. This photograph was taken from the balcony looking toward the pulpit platform and baptistry. The remains of the louvered organ sound chamber may be seen at the upper left. *Nacogdoches* Daily Sentinel.

"STEVE AND I CAME TO NACOGDOCHES AND VISITED FIRST BAPTIST CHURCH IN 1952, AS STUDENTS AT SFA. WE WATCHED THE FIRE IN 1954 FROM ACROSS THE STREET IN THE PIGGLY WIGGLY PARKING LOT AND ATTENDED CHURCH IN THE TABERNACLE, BUT DIDN'T BECOME MEMBERS AND ACTIVE PARTICIPANTS UNTIL WE WERE MARRIED IN 1956. THROUGH THE YEARS THERE WERE SPECIAL SUNDAY SCHOOL TEACHERS SUCH AS MRS. ROSALEE CURTIS, MRS. SAM STRIPLING, MRS. JOHN RUDISILL, AND MRS. FRANK HATHCOCK."

Luegene Crow

Wheeless, the education and music director, recalled that he had been able to save his music library and some of the office equipment before the fire reached them, but the recently repaired pipe organ and the new grand piano in the auditorium were lost. Cartlidge was not so fortunate. He lost his entire library, including twenty years of sermons. A small Hammond electric organ that had recently been returned to the church after a city-wide, month-long tent revival was also a casualty of the fire. Items that were rescued included the pulpit Bible and the pulpit from the auditorium of the old wooden church. Frances (Mrs. John) Rudisill saved the original communion service by entering the burning building and snatching it from its storage place.

The morning after the fire, many church members recalled a statement made by the pastor in the Wednesday evening prayer meeting preceding the fire. Most remembered it as, "What this church needs is to be set on fire for the Lord,"[3] while others recalled what was said as, "What this church needs is a good fire of concern."[4] Regardless of what Cartlidge's exact words were, he had to endure a great deal of good-natured teasing from members of his congregation and the townspeople about the Lord granting his wish.

Eddie Martin Revival

Two young revival attendees were eager to get evangelist Eddie Martin's autograph in their Bibles. *First Baptist Church Archives.*

During the first two-thirds of the twentieth century, tent meetings were commonly held in East Texas communities. In June 1952, First Baptist Church joined with other congregations in the city to sponsor Eddie Martin, an evangelist from Lancaster, Pennsylvania, in a three-week meeting conducted in a tent "cathedral" erected on a vacant lot on the southwest corner of East Austin and North Pecan streets. All of the city's Baptist congregations, joined by several other denominations, sponsored the meeting. Jared Cartlidge, in his second pastorate of First Baptist Church, chaired the campaign committee. An opening night crowd of 2,000 soon grew to an overflow crowd of 3,400, reported by the *Daily Sentinel* to be the largest revival attendance in the city's history. Earlier in the afternoon, prior to the service, a group met at First Baptist Church to pray for one hundred conversions. When the invitation was given that night, 104 individuals responded. This was the largest and one of the last tent revivals held in Nacogdoches.

On one Sunday evening, a record crowd of almost 4,000 attended the Eddie Martin services and overflowed the revival tent. *Nacogdoches* Daily Sentinel.

On the Monday following the Wednesday night fire that gutted the sanctuary in July 1953, the men of First Baptist, under the direction of A. J. (Whitey) Thompson, began construction of a tabernacle to house the congregation's worship services. Located north of the sanctuary on church property behind the Hardeman house, the tabernacle was an open-sided shed with a sawdust floor. Benches constructed by the men of the church and folding chairs salvaged from the burned-out building provided seating. The tabernacle was completed in four days, and worship services were held in it until the rebuilt sanctuary was completed in October 1954. *Nacogdoches Daily Sentinel.*

"THE TABERNACLE WAS A TEMPORARY WOODEN STRUCTURE WITH OPEN SIDES AND SAWDUST FLOORS. I ENJOYED GOING TO CHURCH IN THE TABERNACLE, ESPECIALLY SUNDAY EVENINGS WHEN WE SANG GOSPEL MUSIC IN THE OPEN-AIR ATMOSPHERE. IT WAS OVER A YEAR BEFORE WE MOVED BACK INTO THE CHURCH AFTER RESTORATION WAS COMPLETED IN OCTOBER 1954."

Delores (Sutton) Jenkins

Other churches of the city were quick to offer the use of their facilities, but the congregation decided that they would erect a tabernacle on church property as they had during the original construction of the destroyed auditorium. Within four days the men of the church completed an open-sided tabernacle at the rear of the frame house the church owned on its north side. The tabernacle was floored with sawdust, leading the congregation to "laughingly call themselves saints in the sawdust."[5] Folding chairs salvaged from the church basement, supplemented by benches, provided seating. Several large box fans that survived the fire provided cooling, but the tabernacle was still hot in the summer and cold in the winter. The two frame houses the church owned on either side, along with the Scout Hut under the hill at the rear of the church, provided temporary meeting space for Sunday school classes and the Training Union.

Testing revealed that the fourteen-inch exterior walls were still sound and could be used to rebuild the auditorium. By August 12, the original plans for a $250,000 extension of the education building were expanded to $450,000 to include rebuilding the auditorium. The original architect of the brick auditorium, Hal Tucker, was hired to oversee its reconstruction and design the new addition. By the end of the year, local building contractor Ellis Kingham and Son was at work rebuilding the destroyed portions of the church plant. Difficulties in securing the necessary structural steel slowed the process, and rebuilding the damaged portions of the building was not completed until October 1954.

The dramatic fires that damaged and then destroyed the auditorium had a tendency to overshadow the progress the church made in other areas during Cartlidge's second pastorate. Before either fire occurred, plans were underway to expand the educational facilities of the church. After the fires these plans were resurrected. The only difference was the addition of the rebuilding of the damaged portions of the church plant.

In a continuation of the church's support of the college student ministry, ground was broken in 1952 for a new $50,000 home for the Baptist Student Union on East College Street. First Baptist Church, along with the other Baptist churches of the city, played a major role in securing the building by pledging $8,500 toward its construction. This building served the BSU for fifty years.

By 1953, West Side Mission, established by First Baptist in 1948, was ready to operate as an independent church. It was renamed Memorial Baptist Church and was given title to its building and land by First Baptist for "as long as it cooperated with the Baptist General Convention of Texas."[6] In 2001 it began operating as Iglesia Bautista Memorial to minister to the spiritual needs of the city's growing Hispanic population.

Cartlidge continued the congregation's tradition of holding frequent revivals, preaching some himself and inviting guest evangelists to conduct others. In 1953 he served as the general chairman of a three-week, citywide revival preached by Eddie Martin, an evangelist from Lancaster, Pennsylvania. The meeting, sponsored by the Baptist churches of Nacogdoches and several congregations of other denominations in the city, drew record crowds of four thousand in a large tent erected on the southwest corner of East Austin and North Pecan streets.

On June 27, 1954, slightly less than a year after the second fire, Cartlidge resigned to accept the position of administrator of the Texas Baptist Children's Home in Round Rock, Texas. He had served as chairman of its board since the home's founding in 1950. His resignation was effective July 4 while the church was still meeting in the sawdust of the tabernacle. The congregation remembered him as a warm-hearted individual

In 1952, First Baptist led in securing funding for a new facility to house the growing Baptist Student Union ministry at Stephen F. Austin State College. Shown turning the first shovels of dirt to begin construction are the BSU president W. L. (Bill) Bain and W. B. (Bill) Coble, BSU director. *First Baptist Church Archives.*

A new building to house the Baptist Student Union was constructed in 1952 on the site previously occupied by the two-story frame house on East College Street that originally housed the BSU. Just as for the BSU's first home, First Baptist Church played a major role in securing the new facility. *First Baptist Church Archives.*

who loved sports, especially Baylor University football. Following his time at the Texas Baptist Children's Home, he served as pastor of the First Baptist Church of Gilmer, Texas, and later as vice president for development for East Texas Baptist College in Marshall, Texas. In 1967, Cartlidge returned to Nacogdoches and First Baptist to serve as area missionary for the Shelby-'Doches Baptist Association. During his time as missionary, his office was located in First Baptist. After his retirement Cartlidge returned to Gilmer where he died in 1979.

Immediately following Cartlidge's resignation, a pulpit committee was appointed to seek a new pastor. Meanwhile, preachers who were not considered prospects were scheduled to fill the pulpit. On Sunday, July 18, William H. Crook, a graduate student at Southwestern Baptist Theological Seminary in Fort Worth, Texas, was the supply preacher. The congregation was so impressed with him that even before he delivered the evening message some were saying that the pulpit committee, chaired by Elbert Reese, did not need to look any further.

On August 1, Crook was invited to return and preach in view of a possible call to serve as pastor of the church. One current church member, Jeanette Williams, who was also Crook's niece, was present and described the experience:

> On a very hot August weekend, my family and I were visiting a relative in Lufkin. Upon our arrival we were informed that Bill Crook, my mother's brother, was the guest speaker at First Baptist Church in Nacogdoches on Sunday. We decided to surprise the Crooks by attending the service. The church had burned, and services were being held in a huge tent [tabernacle] with sawdust on the floor. After the sermon we

The third mission church established by First Baptist was West Side Baptist Mission. When the mission became a self-supporting church in 1953, its name was changed to Memorial Baptist Church. In 1994, the church reorganized into a Spanish-language church, Iglesia Bautista Memorial, to accommodate the growing Hispanic population of Nacogdoches. *Photo by Tom Atchison.*

were waiting to visit briefly with Bill and Eleanor when Mr. J. T. Cox came by us in his ever-happy, smiling demeanor and said as he shook hands with Eleanor, "Well, I don't know about you, but I'm going to vote for that young man."[7]

The congregation extended Crook a call to pastor the church and he accepted on the condition that he be allowed sufficient time off during the next two years to complete the dissertation for his ThD degree.

Crook's first Sunday as pastor was August 22, 1954. Eleanor, his wife, recorded in her diary that on that Sunday, "The rain came down in torrents on the tabernacle, causing those near the sides to move in. Several hundred waited to meet us at the end of the service—we love them already. They are a very warm and responsive people, and the spirit of the service was one of rejoicing in the sure way God has led pastor and people together."[8]

A native of Illinois, Crook was the son and grandson of Baptist ministers. He was graduated from Aransas Pass High School, and following his service as an Air Force engineer/gunner in World War II, he was graduated from Baylor University in Waco, Texas. While attending Baylor, he was ordained into the ministry at Seventh and James Baptist Church in Waco, and then attended Southwestern Baptist Seminary in Fort Worth.

Crook considered his first duty as a minister was to preach the Word. He was an excellent speaker who devoted much time to study and sermon

Bill Parmer, Church Historian

William Tellis (Bill) Parmer joined First Baptist Church in 1924 during the pastorate of The Reverend Bonnie Grimes. Serving overseas in the armed forces in World War II, Parmer suffered an injury that confined him to a wheelchair for the remainder of his life. In spite of Parmer's disability, he faithfully attended the services of First Baptist Church, and in 1955 the congregation ordained him as a deacon. During the pastorate of Bill Crook, Parmer edited *The Pastor's Call*, a bimonthly newsletter written by Crook for shut-in members of the congregation. At Crook's urging, Parmer researched and wrote the history of the church's first seventy-five years. His *Seventy-five Years in Nacogdoches: A History of the First Baptist Church, 1884–1959* was published as part of the church's celebration of its seventy-fifth anniversary in 1959. *First Baptist Church Archives.*

William H. (Bill) Crook was the seventeenth minister to pastor First Baptist Church. Crook was a supply preacher for the church following Jared Cartlidge's resignation in the summer of 1954. The congregation was so impressed with the young seminary graduate student that they issued a call for him to pastor the church. He and his wife, the former Eleanor Butt, quickly endeared themselves to the church family. *First Baptist Church Archives.*

preparation. Church members at the time remember that he preached his sermons into a tape recorder and played them back to himself, often as he drove the quiet streets at night. His wife recalled that he had a flair for the dramatic in his sermons, sometimes using titles related to popular songs of the time such as "Who Stepped On My Blue Suede Shoes?" and "What's Behind the Green Door?" Once in a sermon about Jesus' teachings on forgiving others, Crook brought out a large stone, placed it on the pulpit, and ended his message by stating, "Let him who is without sin among you cast the first stone." The stone remained on the pulpit for the next six years. Periodically, Crook would pick it up and ask the congregation, "Is there anyone here who would like to throw this stone?"[9]

When the Crooks moved into the parsonage at 801 North Street, the house was already almost seventy-five years old. Despite fresh paint and new carpet and linoleum, it still left much to be desired, so when the two-story brick home of Mrs. Orland Patton, located on Garner Street, became available in late 1956, the church purchased it. Known as The Oaks, the new parsonage was an ideal location for church picnics, fellowships, receptions, and the growing Crook family.

One of the first tasks to face Crook as the church's pastor was to complete the construction project begun under Cartlidge and get the congregation out of the sawdust in the tabernacle. The renovation of the main building was completed in October 1954, and Crook moved quickly to get construction of the new north and south wings underway. These additions

Shortly after the arrival of Bill Crook as pastor of First Baptist, the congregation replaced the old frame parsonage on North Street with a two-story brick house on Garner Street. Named "The Oaks" for the large oak trees that dominated its yard, the home housed the growing Crook family and provided a pleasant setting for church picnics and other gatherings. *First Baptist Church Archives.*

Construction of the north and south wings following the fire in 1953 required clearing the lots to the north and south of the main church building. During the construction phase, the South Annex was moved west of the main facility down the hillside where it continued to provide meeting space for the youth Sunday school and Training Union classes. *Nacogdoches* Daily Sentinel.

were designed to provide classroom space for the Sunday school and Training Union programs, a new kitchen and fellowship hall, and a chapel, parlor, and student lounge. The contractor for the additions, J. A. Nesbit, completed the work late in 1955. On Sunday, February 4, 1956, a special service of dedication and an open house was held at 3:00 p.m. Dr. W. R. White, president of Baylor University, delivered the dedicatory message. After vows of dedication by the pastor and congregation, The Reverend A. T. Garrard, senior Nacogdoches County Baptist minister and pastor of Old North Church, pronounced the benediction.

With the newly expanded facilities in place, the congregation was ready for Crook to lead them in expanding all programs of the church. The music and educational ministries were separated, and individuals employed to lead each program. A youth director and a building engineer were employed, and a full-time business manager and secretary to the pastor were hired to systemize the church records.

Crook placed strong emphasis on ministering to the students of Stephen F. Austin State College and aimed his Sunday evening messages directly at them. As a result, First Baptist became known as "the student's church."[10] In the spring of 1956, a weeklong Laymen's Revival, led by eight college students, resulted in 250 conversions and rededications of high school and college students. The song leader of the revival, Bill McWhorter, met

The Building Committee members who oversaw the rebuilding and expansion of church facilities from 1953 to 1956, are, front left to right, Dr. B. A. Copass, John J. Rudisill, Frank Shofner, C. S. (Shorty) Jones, J. A. (Jimmy) Partin, and A. J. (Whitey) Thompson. Back row, left to right, J. E. (Elbert) Reese, J. W. Sutton, John Crawford, and M. O. Sutton. *First Baptist Church Archives.*

Following the fire in 1953 that gutted the sanctuary, the congregation rebuilt the destroyed parts of the church plant and added the wings to the north and south, a fellowship hall, and a chapel. *Architect's rendering–First Baptist Church Archives. South view–Tom Atchison.*

his future wife, Shirley Whitton, during this revival. They were married, and after McWhorter completed law school at the University of Texas in Austin, they returned to Nacogdoches and became faithful members of First Baptist.

Five young men were ordained to the gospel ministry by First Baptist during Crook's pastorate. Three of them were ordained in the same year, 1957. They were Herman Hendrix, Richard (Dick) W. McClain, and Gerald Sitton. An additional young church member, Gordon Estell, was licensed to preach by the church during Crook's tenure.

Crook's emphasis on Bible study and evangelism was expressed in numerous Bible studies and revivals held during his pastorate by such notable ministers as Buckner Fanning, Jess Moody, W. M. Shamburger, John Haggai, Dr. J. Sidlow Baxter, and Dr. Donald Grey Barnhouse. Along with his promotion of Bible study and evangelism, Crook built upon the church's longtime concern for world missions by leading the congregation to adopt a missionary to Guatemala, Clark Scanlon, and have his salary paid from First Baptist's contributions to the Southern Baptist Convention's co-operative program.

In the fall of 1955, the church began a new educational venture, a preschool or kindergarten led by Mrs. Edgar (Ina) Eddings, a much-loved teacher who had retired after serving thirty-two years in the Nacogdoches public schools. In announcing the beginning of the school and the employment of Mrs. Eddings as teacher, the chairman of the preschool committee, Marvin McBride, stated, "We want a school that will do more than take the child out of the mother's hair for a few hours. Our purpose is to build Christian character."[11] Providing early childhood education in a Christian environment continues to be the goal of the First Baptist Day School.

In 1959 Crook led the church to commemorate its seventy-fifth anniversary with a celebration. He prevailed upon W. T. Parmer, long the church's unofficial historian, to write a history of the institution. The result was *Seventy-five Years in Nacogdoches: A History of the First Baptist Church, 1884–1959*, published in Dallas by the Dorsey Company. In addition to the publication of the church's history, a special celebration was held in the worship service on Sunday July 26, with more than one thousand members and guests present. Plans called for the special service to be followed by a picnic on the lawn of The Oaks. Rain precluded holding the picnic outdoors, however, so it was held in the church's Fellowship Hall. At the picnic the congregation's oldest member, Hugh B. Davis, was to unveil a commemorative plaque on the large oak tree on the parsonage

Dr. Bill Crook

William H. (Bill) Crook is the only pastor of First Baptist to serve on the national political stage. Following his unsuccessful bid for election to Congress and a stint as president of San Marcos Baptist Academy, Crook was appointed by President Lyndon Johnson as regional director of the Office of Economic Opportunity and later as the national director of the VISTA program. In 1968 Crook was appointed United States ambassador to Australia. The Reverend Crook and son Bill Jr. are shown here with President Johnson.
Courtesy of Eleanor Butt Crook.

In 1959, First Baptist Church celebrated its seventy-fifth anniversary. Joining Dr. Bill Crook (center) and more than one thousand members and guests in the celebration worship service on July 26, 1959, was one of the congregation's oldest members, Hugh Davis (left), and the church's twelfth pastor, C. A. Westbrook (right), who served the congregation from 1914 to 1919. Rain caused the afternoon picnic scheduled at the parsonage to be held in Fellowship Hall. *First Baptist Church Archives.*

Right: The fourth mission church established by First Baptist was Calvary Chapel. When the mission became a self-supporting church in 1959, its name was changed to Calvary Baptist Church. After four decades in its original location on East Main Street, the church relocated to a new facility on Northeast Stallings Drive. *Photo by Tom Atchison.*

lawn. The plaque stated that the church's seventh-fifth anniversary was celebrated under the tree. To ensure that the plaque's statement was accurate, the Crooks hosted another picnic under the tree on a later day.

During his time at First Baptist, Crook encouraged the church to continue establishing missions in parts of the city where there was no Baptist church. In 1956 the church established a new mission church, its fourth, in the eastern quadrant of Nacogdoches known as the Orton Hill neighborhood. A graduate of Stephen F. Austin and Southwestern Baptist Theological Seminary, James Mahoney, agreed to pastor the mission, and First Baptist contributed $3,000 annually for three years to support it financially. The first services of the new mission were held January 13, 1957, in the living room of Mahoney's parents' home located on the corner of West Main and Sweetgum streets. There were forty-three charter

members present. A group of First Baptist men—A. J. Thompson, Willard Sutton, M. O. Sutton, and C. W. Gound—assisted with the purchase of a lot at this location, and by June, First Baptist was making plans to construct a 200-seat auditorium at a cost of $5,000. Two years after it held its first service, Calvary Chapel became Calvary Baptist Church, an independent Baptist church operating in cooperation with the Baptist General Convention of Texas and the Southern Baptist Convention. It continues in another location as one of the larger Baptist congregations in the city.

A fifth mission, Faith Baptist Chapel, grew from a ministry conducted by college students in a neighborhood in the western part of Nacogdoches known as the Ammons Addition. Beginning in the fall of 1954, the students conducted a vacation Bible school for the neighborhood children. Sunday school, Training Union, and preaching services on Thursday evenings were soon added. In March 1957, Herman Hendrix, one of the young ministers newly ordained by Crook, assumed the responsibility of conducting these services on a "faith basis." This gave the mission its name of Faith Baptist Chapel. In May, First Baptist agreed to pay the rent on the building and a salary of $50 per month to Hendrix. In 1958 First Baptist purchased a lot and constructed a new frame building for the mission at a cost of $5,000.

Faith Chapel continued to operate as a mission of First Baptist Church for several years, but it never became a self-supporting church, and the property was later sold.

Crook was active in denominational and associational affairs. He served as moderator of the Shelby-'Doches Baptist Association, president of District II of the Baptist General Convention of Texas, on the Foreign Mission Board of the Southern Baptist Convention, as a trustee of East Texas Baptist College at Marshall, Texas, and

CHARLES FOX HIGH SCHOOL REVIVAL

TIME SCHEDULE

6:15 p.m.—Supper (Monday, Wednesday, Friday)

7:00 p.m.—Y. P. Choir Practice. Prayer time for other age groups (Monday thru Thursday)

7:30 p.m.—Worship Service (Monday thru Thursday)

8:45 p.m.—Seminar or Fellowship (Monday thru Thursday)

6:45 p.m.—Friday Vesper Service

Saturday night—Prayer Service

CHARLES FOX

BILL McWHORTER

FIRST BAPTIST CHURCH – SEPT. 7-14

In September 1958, Bill McWhorter came to First Baptist Church to lead the music in a laymen's youth revival. He accompanied the revival preacher on a date with one of the church members and met his future wife, Shirley Whitton. *First Baptist Church Archives.*

"WHEN I WAS WORKING IN THE CHURCH OFFICE WITH RITA BAINES, EVERYONE WAS TEASING ME BECAUSE A YOUNG MAN WAS COMING TO LEAD THE MUSIC FOR THE YOUTH REVIVAL. I MADE UP MY MIND THAT I DID NOT WANT TO HAVE ANYTHING TO DO WITH HIM. NOW, HERE WE ARE—FORTY-NINE YEARS LATER—ABOUT TO CELEBRATE OUR FIFTIETH WEDDING ANNIVERSARY!"

Shirley (Whitton) McWhorter

First Baptist Day School

In the fall of 1955, under the pastorate of Bill Crook, First Baptist began offering a week-day kindergarten program for five-year-old children. At that time kindergarten classes were all taught in churches or private homes since none were available in the public schools. Mrs. Edgar (Ina) Eddings, a church member and a thirty-two-year veteran teacher in the Nacogdoches public schools who retired at the end of the 1954–1955 school year, was hired as the school's director and teacher. In employing Mrs. Eddings, Marvin McBride, chairman of the school committee, stated: "We believe with Mrs. Eddings as our principal we will have the finest church school in East Texas. We want a school that will do more than take the child out of the mother's way for a few hours. Our purpose is to build Christian character."[1] A photograph of the first class and Mrs. Eddings shows twenty-one pupils. They were Dee Ann Bass, Janet Muckleroy, Jimmy Carpenter, David Monzingo, Sherry Johnston, Mike McGrew, Quin Goodrum, Cathy Schmidt, Robert Robinson, George Middlebrook, Tommy Kendrick, Carol Childers, Jody Stripling, Sandy Poe, David Norton, Travis Whitaker, Rebecca Kellum, Tom Gaston, Lynn Bousman, Sheila Cox, and Linda Sue Miles. The class met in a room in the south wing where the office suite is located in 2009. At the end of the first year, the twenty-one young scholars recited memory verses and sang songs for parents and friends before receiving their diplomas in the church chapel.

After one year Mrs. Ross (Olga) White took over as the school's director and teacher, a position she held for sixteen years. During her tenure the enrollment in the school increased and classes were added for three- and four-year-old children. In the fall of 1957, a day nursery was added to assist working mothers. Nursery hours were from 7:15 a.m. until

Mrs. Ina Eddings, the first teacher and director of First Baptist Church's Day School, and some of her first class of kindergartners display gingerbread men they made as part of their lessons. *Nacogdoches* Daily Sentinel.

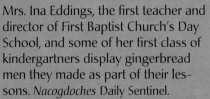

Mrs. Olga White, the second teacher and director of the Day School, and her first class of pupils in 1956. *First Baptist Church Archives.*

5:15 p.m. Children were accepted from infancy up to school age, and four- and five-year-olds could attend the kindergarten class in the mornings at no additional charge. A noon meal, as well as nutritious morning and afternoon snacks, was served. Mrs. Doyle (Bettye) Alexander was the nursery leader. In 1973, Mrs. White retired and was honored with a reception attended by many of her former pupils. Of her time at the school, Mrs. White said, "It has been one of my greatest blessings."[2]

Following Mrs. White's retirement, Claudette Sutton, one of the Day School teachers, was named director. After she resigned to accept a teaching position with the Nacogdoches public schools in 1975, Ken Etley, the church's minister of education and administration, assumed the director's duties. In 1978, when Etley resigned, Peggy Partin, a teacher in the school, was given the additional responsibility of directing the program. Partin served in this capacity for twenty years until she retired in 1998. During this time the school had two classes each for three-year-old, four-year-old, and five-year-old children and moved into new facilities in the primary wing constructed in conjunction with the Christian Life Center. Later, the school occupied space in the Children's Building. Diedra Sutton followed Partin as director. Laurie Rogers was the director of the school in 2008–2009.

During the last decade of the twentieth century and the first decade of the twenty-first century, an increase in the number of private and church preschool and kindergarten programs and the availability of state-funded programs in public school resulted in decreased enrollments in the Day School. By the fall of 2008, it became evident that continuing the school was no longer economically feasible, and the church regretfully decided to end the program at the conclusion of the 2008–2009 academic year.

Mrs. Peggy Partin, Day School teacher and director, works with two of her students. *First Baptist Church Archives.*

First Baptist Day School students and teachers in 2008. Teachers shown at right are, front row (left to right), Ann Wimberly and Jo Ann Hebert; second row, Kristi Caldwell; third row, Laurie Rogers (teacher and director); and fourth row, Ronna Simon.

1. Nacogdoches *Daily Sentinel*, undated clipping in First Baptist Church Archives.
2. *The Baptist Standard*, First Baptist Church Edition, May 16, 1973.

In 1957, First Baptist Church established a fifth mission, Faith Chapel, in the Ammons Addition. Like the Bonaldo Mission, Faith Chapel never became a self-supporting church and was discontinued after a few years. *First Baptist Church Archives.*

Bill Crook Tells 'Why'

Tonight,

(Monday)

At 8:30

KTRE-TV

Channel 9

BILL CROOK

On January 24, 1960, Bill Crook ended his 5½-year pastorate of First Baptist Church when he resigned to enter the race for Congress. Crook told his congregation that his decision to enter the race was the result of his growing conviction that Christianity would work in politics, and he went on television to explain his reasons to the public. *Nacogdoches Daily Sentinel.*

on numerous other denominational and associational boards and committees. Under his leadership the church hosted associational meetings and the District II Baptist General Convention of Texas convention. In addition, Crook was much in demand as a speaker, preaching revivals, conducting Bible studies, and delivering lectures at Southwestern Baptist Theological Seminary. His wife, Eleanor, was a strong supporter of his pastoral ministry, teaching the college women's Sunday school class, leading in the Women's Missionary Union, and opening her home to college students and church members alike.

Local community affairs did not escape Crook's attention. He led a local coalition of churches to campaign against the sale of comic books, worked for the reduction of electricity rates for churches, defended the Baptist practice of fellowship meals, and supported the location of a proposed naval training base in Nacogdoches County. His interest in local governmental affairs was, perhaps, a foreshadowing of a greater involvement in government and politics at the national level. On Sunday, January 24, 1960, Crook read his letter of resignation to the deacons in a special called meeting at 9:00 a.m. and later to the entire congregation in the morning worship service. He explained that his resignation was for the purpose of entering the race for representative of the Seventh Congressional District of Texas. He said his decision was not made hastily, but after a long period of "growing awareness of the need for men who have succeeded in other areas of enterprise to enter the field of statesmanship" and out of a "conviction that Christianity will work in politics and that somebody has to take a chance to prove that conviction."[12] He viewed this step not as leaving the ministry but as an enlargement of his ministry. Crook's bid for a congressional seat was

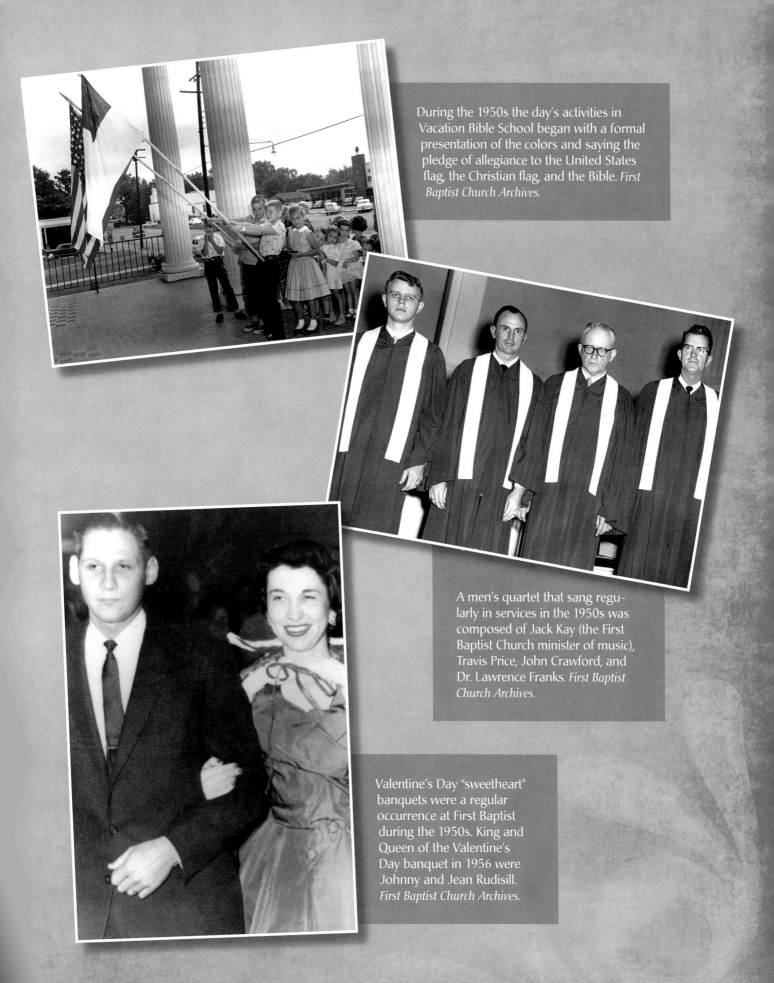

During the 1950s the day's activities in Vacation Bible School began with a formal presentation of the colors and saying the pledge of allegiance to the United States flag, the Christian flag, and the Bible. *First Baptist Church Archives.*

A men's quartet that sang regularly in services in the 1950s was composed of Jack Kay (the First Baptist Church minister of music), Travis Price, John Crawford, and Dr. Lawrence Franks. *First Baptist Church Archives.*

Valentine's Day "sweetheart" banquets were a regular occurrence at First Baptist during the 1950s. King and Queen of the Valentine's Day banquet in 1956 were Johnny and Jean Rudisill. *First Baptist Church Archives.*

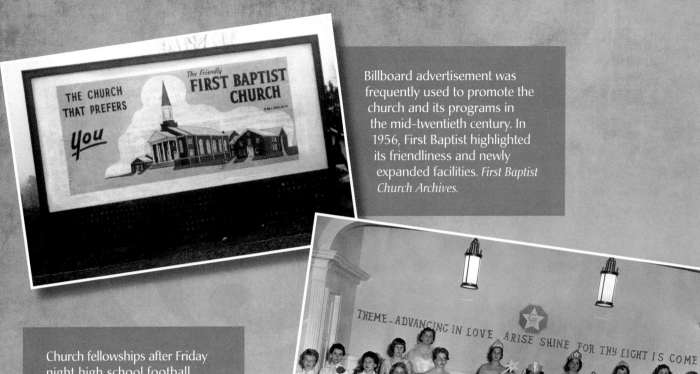

Billboard advertisement was frequently used to promote the church and its programs in the mid-twentieth century. In 1956, First Baptist highlighted its friendliness and newly expanded facilities. *First Baptist Church Archives.*

Church fellowships after Friday night high school football games provided a Christian atmosphere for friends to get together and celebrate victories and mourn losses. Shown here in an after-game fellowship in 1958, are, left to right, Dave Ward (foreground, First Baptist Church minister of education), Steve Scott, Glenda Tipton, Rose Mary Ard, Mary Gayle McKewen, Helen Palmer, Nelwyn Simons, Sue Braselton, Dana Henley, Darla Whitton, Nancy Weatherly, and Linda Reese. *Nacogdoches* Daily Sentinel.

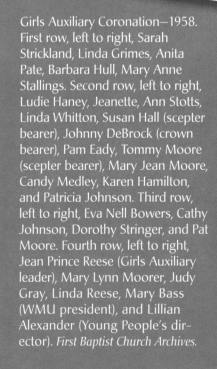

Girls Auxiliary Coronation—1958. First row, left to right, Sarah Strickland, Linda Grimes, Anita Pate, Barbara Hull, Mary Anne Stallings. Second row, left to right, Ludie Haney, Jeanette, Ann Stotts, Linda Whitton, Susan Hall (scepter bearer), Johnny DeBrock (crown bearer), Pam Eady, Tommy Moore (scepter bearer), Mary Jean Moore, Candy Medley, Karen Hamilton, and Patricia Johnson. Third row, left to right, Eva Nell Bowers, Cathy Johnson, Dorothy Stringer, and Pat Moore. Fourth row, left to right, Jean Prince Reese (Girls Auxiliary leader), Mary Lynn Moorer, Judy Gray, Linda Reese, Mary Bass (WMU president), and Lillian Alexander (Young People's director). *First Baptist Church Archives.*

unsuccessful, but he soon had the opportunity to prove that Christianity would work in politics, albeit in appointed rather than elected positions.

After losing the election, Crook became involved in education, government service, and business. He served the next five years as president of San Marcos Baptist Academy. In 1965 President Lyndon Johnson appointed him regional director of the Office of Economic Opportunity in Austin, Texas. Two years later he was tapped to serve the Johnson administration as national director of the VISTA program in Washington, D.C. In 1968 he was named United States ambassador to Australia where he and his family proved to be extremely popular with the Australians. Crook's time in San Marcos meant that the city would be considered home for the remainder of his life, and he returned there in 1970 to pursue various business interests while continuing to work in humanitarian and governmental initiatives. At his death in 1997, Crook's friend, journalist Bill Moyers, paid him the following tribute: "He was a man of deep faith who concealed his piety from the public. He loved the world of ideas and was at home in every book he read. He was about as whole a human being as I've ever known, and to top it off, he had a wicked wit. Consider yourself lucky if you have a friend like him—just one."[13]

Following Crook's resignation the church lost no time in selecting a pulpit committee to seek his replacement. After the church voted on the motion to accept the resignation, Dr. Ben A. Copass, chairman of the deacons, announced to the congregation that they should come to the evening service prepared to vote on a pulpit committee. They did, and a nine-member committee began work the next day.

"I HAVE READ MANY ACCOUNTS OF PASTORS' WIVES MADE MISERABLE BY DIFFICULT, DEMANDING CONGREGATIONS, BUT I FOUND NOTHING OTHER THAN KINDNESS AND NURTURE [AT FIRST BAPTIST]. OUR FIRST TWO CHILDREN WERE BORN DURING THESE YEARS, AND BILL JR., OUR OLDEST, REMEMBERS SUNDAY SCHOOL WITH RUTH [WILLIAMSON] AND HAZEL AND MIMI [WHITEHEAD], THOUGH HE WAS ONLY FOUR WHEN WE LEFT."

Eleanor Butt Crook

1. Jaramy (Cartlidge) Karns to Jean Rudisill, July 27, 2008.

2. Carolyn R. Ericson, *Fires and Firemen of Nacogdoches* (Nacogdoches, TX: Ericson Books, 1976), p. 173.

3. W. T. Parmer, *Seventy-five Years in Nacogdoches: A History of the First Baptist Church, 1884–1959* (Dallas, TX: Dorsey Co., 1959), p. 118.

4. William H. Wheeless to Allen Reed, undated.

5. Johnny Rudisill, interview with Jean Rudisill, April 8, 2008; Shirley McWhorter, interview with Jean Rudisill, April 22, 2008.

6. Parmer, *op. cit.*, p. 119.

7. Jeanette Williams, untitled MS, June 2008.

8. Eleanor Butt Crook, "Recollections," MS, April 29, 2008.

9. Ibid.

10. Rita Baines, "William H. Crook," MS, undated.

11. *Daily Sentinel*, undated clipping in the First Baptist Church archives.

12. *Daily Sentinel*, January 25, 1960.

13. San Marcos *Daily Record*, October 30, 1997.

5

An Expectant and Responsive Congregation

"Every Sunday has been a joy as I stepped into the pulpit to minister to an expectant and responsive congregation."

Bill R. Austin

*F*OUR MONTHS AFTER BILL CROOK RESIGNED FROM FIRST BAPTIST Church to run for Congress, the church called a new pastor, the Reverend W. Edwin Crawford. Crawford was invited by the pulpit committee chaired by Elbert Reese to preach in view of a call on Sunday, May 1, 1960. The following Sunday morning, May 8, the congregation voted unanimously to call him as its new pastor. He telegraphed his acceptance that afternoon, saying that he would be on the job June 1 and preach in both services on Sunday, June 5. When he told his friend, *Houston Chronicle* sports writer Morris Frank, about the pulpit committee from First Baptist, Crawford quipped, "I think some of them are your old cronies," referring to Elbert Reese, A. J. (Whitey) Thompson, and John Crawford, who were friends of Frank in his East Texas days.[1]

Crawford was born in Temple, Texas. He was a graduate of Temple High School, Temple Junior College, and Baylor University. Following his graduation from Baylor University, he attended the United States Chaplain School at Harvard University and served as an Army chaplain in the European Theatre during World War II. After Crawford's military service,

Opposite: W. Edwin Crawford was the eighteenth individual to serve as pastor of First Baptist Church. He was serving as pastor of Houston West End Baptist Church in Houston, Texas, when he was called to come to First Baptist Church. *First Baptist Church Archives.*

he was graduated from Southwestern Baptist Theological Seminary. At the time he was called to pastor First Baptist, Crawford was serving as pastor of Houston West End Baptist Church in Houston, Texas, where he had been since 1956. Previously he served as associate pastor of South Main Baptist Church in Houston, Texas, and as associate pastor of the First Baptist Church of Paris, Texas. During his student days, Crawford pastored Pendleton, Elm Grove, and Prairie Dell Baptist churches.

When the Crawfords arrived in Nacogdoches, they found a congregation still somewhat in shock from having a pastor leave the ministry to run for political office. In addition, there was some lingering disagreement over the purchase of the new parsonage, an outstanding church debt of $165,000, and a bank account in the red. Crawford immediately began to work on renewing the fellowship among church members, improving the financial condition of the church, and helping the congregation build for the future. His first sermon on Sunday, June 5, titled "Let Us Go On," encouraged the people to leave the past behind and move forward with the work of the church.

One of the initial tasks demanding Crawford's attention was completing the installation of the elevator the church had purchased with funds raised as part of its seventy-fifth anniversary celebration. When Crawford arrived, the elevator was "just hanging there."[2] This was brought to Crawford's attention in his first meeting with the deacons when W. T. (Bill) Parmer, the church's wheelchair-bound historian, brought it up. Crawford immediately agreed with Parmer that the installation should be finished and began the process that evening. He did not learn until later that there was controversy in the church over the elevator, and the chairman of the board of deacons opposed it. After the elevator was operational, Crawford observed, "Sometimes it was best *not* to know *everything*."[3]

In 1963 the Southern Baptist Convention encouraged member churches to send staff members to

Many Nacogdoches churches conducted annual vacation Bible schools after public school dismissed for the summer. Since different denominational churches held their Bible schools at different times, community children often attended several Bible schools during the course of a summer. The children and workers for one First Baptist school in the 1960s are shown with the church's pastor, Edwin Crawford (top row, third from left by white column), on the front steps of the church. *First Baptist Church Archives.*

Opposite: Participating in the Girls Auxiliary coronation service in 1964 were, front row, left to right, Margie Hopper, Alva Ann Hill, Susan Wallace, Janice Geldmier, Patricia Wardlaw, and Sharon Cordell. On the back row are, left to right, Sarah Strickland, Nancy Jones, Julie Hickerson, Rhote Hudgins, Rosemary Williams, Carol Jones, Marilyn Mann, Becky Cordell, Stacy Todd, unknown, and Jeannie Hand. The globe at the rear with a picture of Christ superimposed was made by the pastor's wife, Inez Crawford. *First Baptist Church Archives.*

Japan to help with conducting the Japanese New Life Movement. Crawford wanted First Baptist to participate, but there was no staff to send. Instead Crawford held a pastor-led revival and donated the $1,500 love offering he received to help fund this work.

Under L. E. Lamb's pastorate, First Baptist began to acquire property adjacent to the church to be used for future expansion. Crawford continued this practice, and in 1963 the church purchased the blacksmith shop owned by A. T. Mast on the flood plain west of the church. One member of the congregation recalled that Joe Jones, the church's building engineer, had worked for Mast previously and had a good relationship with him. Jones visited with his former employer and, in his words, "softened him up" on the sale. As a result, when Johnny Rudisill approached Mast on behalf of the church, Mast agreed to sell the property to the church for its appraised value on the tax rolls.[4]

Crawford was a good administrator and sought to maintain the church on a sound financial footing. This included leading the congregation in 1964 to pay off the note on the new parsonage a year before it was due. One year later the church was able to eliminate its remaining debt on the renovation of the burned-out auditorium and the north and south wing additions, leading one deacon to comment with relief, "I never thought we would make it."[5] By the time Crawford left First Baptist in 1967, the church was free of debt and enjoyed a positive balance in its bank account.

THIS DO   IN REMEMBRANCE   OF ME

A former baseball catcher, Crawford was an avid sports fan, especially of the Baylor Bears. After his move to Nacogdoches, he quickly became a strong supporter of the local high school and college teams. Whenever there was a home game, he could be seen in the stands cheering for the Nacogdoches High School Dragons and the Lumberjacks of Stephen F. Austin.

First Baptist Church has a long tradition of performing special musical programs at Christmas. The Sanctuary Choir presented *The Christ Child* by Hawley on December 13, 1964. First row, left to right: Mrs. W. C. Burgess, Hila Sue Fitch, unknown, Bettye Alexander, Noel Thompson, Helen Faye Lewis, LaVerne Cordell, Lucylle Fulmer, unknown, Olga White, Virginia Hill, and Golda Moorer. Second row: Carol Ann Birmingham (pianist), unknown, unknown, unknown, unknown, Alyene Britton, Opal Ann King, Roxie Lowery, Mrs. John Decker, Carmen LaPere, Jo Anna Bentley, Mary Christopher, Doxie McClary. Third row: Henry Middlebrook, George Thompson, Gerald LaPere, Travis Price, D. N. Hull, John Crawford, Joe Robbins, Herschel Fulmer, Emory Johnson, unknown, Ray Summers (organist). *First Baptist Church Archives.*

Inez Crawford assisted her husband with his ministry by being a gracious hostess and becoming involved in the church's organizations. Mrs. Crawford had a special interest in the Women's Missionary Union and encouraged more women to become involved in its work. By the end of her husband's pastorate, enrollment in the WMU had doubled, and nine circles provided daytime and evening meeting options. Mrs. Crawford worked two mornings each week as a volunteer in the Memorial Hospital Auxiliary, where she started a library and book cart for patients. This was one of her favorite activities, and her enjoyment of it prompted another church member, Annette (Mrs. John) Crawford, to volunteer to take her place when she and the Reverend Crawford left Nacogdoches.

The Crawfords were the parents of two sons, Dan and Bob. When they moved to Nacogdoches, Dan had just been graduated from high school and Bob was eight years old. While in college Dan surrendered to preach, and, as pastor, his father had the privilege of ordaining his son to the gospel ministry on December 1, 1963.

Throughout his career, Crawford was actively involved in denominational affairs. At various times he served as a trustee of Southwestern Baptist Theological Seminary in Fort Worth, Texas, on the executive board of the Baptist General Convention of Texas, on the executive committee of the Southern Baptist Convention, and as trustee of Houston Baptist College and East Texas Baptist College.

Seven years after accepting the call of First Baptist, Crawford resigned, effective June 15, 1967, to become superintendent of missions for the Golden Triangle Baptist Association. His seven-year pastorate was the fourth-longest in First Baptist history. As he looked back on his time at First Baptist, Crawford recounted that he had received 923 new members, baptized 149 individuals, performed sixty-five weddings, and conducted

101 funerals. On his last Sunday in Nacogdoches, Crawford baptized two converts from the morning service and then led the congregation in observing the Lord's Supper. In his resignation letter, he encouraged the church to continue to move forward for the work of the Kingdom. "The First Baptist Church of Nacogdoches has a great future," he said. "This must not be a time of letting down. We must all work to make this a forward step for every phase of the Kingdom work to which we are committed."[6]

Following his tenure as superintendent of missions for the Golden Triangle Association, Crawford became Director of Development for Southwestern Baptist Theological Seminary. As a former trustee of the institution, he was aware of its needs and in a unique position to secure resources to meet them. He later stated, "finding and developing friends for the seminary was his most significant long-range effort."[7] When Crawford retired from his seminary position at the end of 1983, he returned to his hometown of Temple, Texas. During retirement he continued to assist the seminary as a development consultant, served several churches as interim pastor, preached, and led Together

The Girls Auxiliary coronation service in 1967 recognized members who completed the requirements of the rank of queen. Queens crowned in the September 1967 coronation service are shown with their crown bearers in the church sanctuary. The queens (on the back row, left to right) are Ann Davison, Patricia Wardlaw, Alva Hill, Margie Hooper, Sherrie Sweat, and Janice Geldmier. Their crown bearers standing in front are, left to right, Lisa Rudisill, Patricia Redfield, Kelly Foster, Janice Lewis, Don Sweat, and Stacy Stanaland. *First Baptist Church Archives.*

Through the years First Baptist Church has been a strong supporter of scouting, sponsoring Troop 103 and providing the Scout Hut for the troop's meeting place. Lucylle Fulmer pins the God and Country Award on Barham Fulmer while Herschel Fulmer looks on. *First Baptist Church Archives.*

We Build programs until his death on December 29, 2002. At his funeral Kerry Horn, who grew up in First Baptist during Crawford's pastorate, said when facing problems in his own ministry that he was guided by one question: "What would Brother Crawford do?"[8]

While working on his doctorate at Eastern Baptist Theological Seminary, Dr. Harold Fickett, who had served First Baptist as interim pastor between the tenure of Bonnie Grimes and Jared Cartlidge, became acquainted with a young undergraduate student named Robert (Bob) G. Graves. Fickett was impressed with Graves' preaching ability, had followed his career as a minister, and recommended him to the pulpit committee charged with securing a replacement for Crawford. The committee agreed, and the church called Graves to become the nineteenth minister to serve as pastor of First Baptist.

Graves served First Baptist from December 1, 1967, to January 9, 1972. He grew up in Binghamton, New York, and was graduated from Binghamton Central High School. He earned bachelor's and master's degrees from Eastern Baptist College and Seminary in Philadelphia, Pennsylvania, and Temple University School of Theology, also in Philadelphia. Prior to coming to First Baptist Church, Graves pastored Baptist churches in Huntington Valley, Pennsylvania; Clifton, New Jersey; Bangor, Maine; and Kenova, West Virginia. For three years immediately preceding accepting the call of First Baptist, he worked as a full-time evangelist.

Moving from New England to East Texas was a major change for the Graves family. Their children, Gordon, a college student, Keith, a junior in high school, and Beth, ten years old, were not happy about leaving their friends behind and moving to Texas, but they soon adjusted and made new friends.

During Crawford's pastorate, church organist Barbara Reid and her husband Bunkie, with their children, Leslie, Kathy, and Libba, gave First Baptist a set of hand bells, and Reid organized a ladies hand bell choir. Members were, front row, left to right, Ann Sweat, Noel Thompson, Inez Crawford, Jean Rudisill, Mary Neal Grimland, Dimple Gound, and Barbara Reid (director). Second row, left to right: Laura Lee Horn, Helen Faye Lewis, Rose Ann Pool, Phyllis Iglinsky, Carol Ann Birmingham, and Bettye Alexander. *First Baptist Church Archives.*

As pastor of First Baptist, Bob Graves strongly emphasized the church's responsibility to minister to the students of Stephen F. Austin State University. During his tenure as pastor, a university student choir, the Sound Generation, made recordings and gave concerts locally and on tour. Music minister Earl Davis is shown in a dark blazer in the right foreground kneeling by the car. *First Baptist Church Archives.*

Bob Graves was the nineteenth pastor of First Baptist Church. He served from 1967 to 1972. Prior to accepting the call to pastor First Baptist, Graves was in full-time evangelism and lived in Bangor, Maine. The Graves family shown left to right are daughters-in law Jan and Judy, grandson Shane, Shirley and Bob. Standing in back, left to right, Gordon Graves, Keith Graves, and Beth Graves. *First Baptist Church Archives.*

Missions continued to be a strong emphasis during Graves' pastorate, and the newly purchased church bus was used to transport a mission team to the Rio Grande area to conduct a Bible school at Los Indios. Here Shirley Graves works with the Los Indios children. *First Baptist Church Archives.*

The First Baptist In Disciples youth choir, led by Larry McFadden, minister of youth and music (far right), sang Christmas music for a meeting of the Nacogdoches Noon Lions Club in December 1971. In Disciples members shown, left to right, are Susan Brown, Yancy Barton, Janie Evans, Mike Ammons, Steve Alexander, Mark King, Charles Lee Thompson, Jim Bob Sweat, and Stephen Bedford. *Nacogdoches* Daily Sentinel.

Stained Glass Windows

The glass in the original windows of the sanctuary constructed in 1942 was a light amber color. Church members recall that when the sun shone through the windows, it cast an amber glow over the auditorium. After the sanctuary was destroyed by fire in July 1953, the replacement windows contained lightly frosted glass that let in more light. The congregation was discussing the possibility of replacing these windows with stained glass Bible scenes when Bob Graves was called as pastor. Graves toured the Holy Land for six weeks just prior to his move to Nacogdoches. On his tour he was impressed by the vibrant colors he saw in the wildflowers. Upon his arrival in Nacogdoches, Graves encouraged the congregation to move forward with its plans for the windows and to incorporate the colors he saw in his tour in the glass of the windows. Individuals and families donated funds for the project, and six of the twelve windows were given as memorials. San Antonio artist Ruth B. Dunn was commissioned to design the windows, and she was encouraged to use the colors and form of the Holy Land wildflowers Graves saw. The Orco Company, also of San Antonio, produced and installed the windows. The twelve windows were completed and dedicated in 1970.

Moses and the Ten Commandments. *Photo by Jonathan Canfield.*

There are four tall windows on each side of the sanctuary. The four on the south depict Old Testament scenes while the four on the north depict New Testament scenes. There are two smaller windows under the balcony that depict the two ordinances of Baptist churches—the ordinance of baptism on the south and the ordinance of the Lord's Supper on the north. Above, in the balcony, two windows depict the symbolism of Christ as alpha and omega, the beginning and the end of all things.

As a part of the church's centennial celebration, longtime church member Ida Keeling created a brochure that included pictures of each window and the Biblical story on which it is based. "Upon entering the auditorium," Miss Keeling stated, "one is conscious of being in a place of worship by the soft glow of twelve stained glass windows. Careful observation reveals that the beauty of these windows lies not in their line and color, but in the story that they tell—the story of man's redemption. The windows depicting Old Testament characters illustrate the plan of redemption as foretold in God's promises; while the windows depicting the major events in the life of Jesus Christ show the fulfillment of those promises." The brochure also explained the Biblical color symbolism of the windows: blue signifies heavenly glory; green represents the earth, the world; black represents evil; gold shows the victory of Jesus Christ; purple represents royalty and the priesthood; and red stands for the sacrifice Christ made for man's sins.

The windows illustrated here are Moses with the tablets of the law, representing God's Old Testament covenant with man, and the nativity of Jesus Christ, representing God's New Testament covenant with man.

The Nativity. *Photo by Jonathan Canfield.*

Bill and Margie Austin came to Nacogdoches from Waco, Texas, where he served as pastor of Calvary Baptist Church. Austin was the congregation's twentieth pastor. Planning for the Christian Life Center began under his leadership. *First Baptist Church Archives.*

Graves was known as an outstanding speaker, a fact recognized early in his career when he received the Russell H. Conwell Memorial Prize for the highest average in public speaking while attending seminary. His style of preaching was especially attractive to university students, and there was a significant increase in the number of students attending services during his pastorate. Graves was a good friend of university coaches Gordon Brown (football), and Marshall Brown (basketball), both of whom were members of First Baptist, and he served as unofficial spiritual leader for the Lumberjack athletic teams. Under his preaching, a member of the Lumberjack football team, Rick Scarborough, surrendered to the ministry and worked the remainder of his time in college directing the church's youth activities. He and the Graves family became close friends, and Graves served as his mentor in the ministry. Like his mentor, Scarborough worked as an evangelist and later pastored churches in Pearland and Nacogdoches, Texas. In 1992, while serving as pastor of the First Baptist Church of Pearland, Texas, Scarborough became increasingly concerned about the lack of Christian involvement in civil government and gained national recognition as he led his congregation to become more active in political issues, especially the way sex education was being taught in the local public schools. In 1998, he founded Vision America, a national organization whose stated mission is to "inform and mobilize pastors and their congregations to become salt and light, becoming pro-active in restoring Judeo-Christian values in America."[9]

Members of the pulpit committee that recommended Bill Austin as the church's pastor were, left to right, Jimmy Partin, Frances Rudisill, Edna Earl Reese, Doyle Alexander, Bill Austin with his wife Margie standing in front of him, Gordon Brown, L. D. Pate, Lucyle Jones, and committee chairman John Sutton. Not pictured is C. S. (Shorty) Jones. *First Baptist Church Archives.*

When Graves received the call from First Baptist, members of the congregation were discussing replacing the clear glass in the auditorium windows with stained glass. Graves encouraged the church to move forward with this project and at the same time to renovate the auditorium and the rest of the church plant. Members gave liberally to the stained glass window fund, and six windows were given by individuals as me-

The twenty-first pastor of First Baptist Church was Paul Lionel Crowell. Crowell came to First Baptist from the First Baptist Church of Leesville, Louisiana. Under Crowell's leadership the plans for the Christian Life Center were finalized and its construction completed. *First Baptist Church Archives.*

morials. Ruth B. Dunn of the Orco Company, the San Antonio, Texas, artist commissioned to design the windows, used photographs Graves took on a trip to the Holy Land in selecting scenes and colors for the windows. They were dedicated in 1970. The four windows on the south side of the auditorium depict the old covenant plan of redemption, as shown by events in the lives of Abraham, Moses, David, and Isaiah, and the four windows on the north depict events in the life of Christ, the new covenant plan of redemption.

His time in evangelism acquainted Graves with many outstanding preachers of the time, and he invited several to conduct revival meetings and Bible conferences at First Baptist. Among these were the Reverend John Haggai and Dr. R. G. Lee, pastor emeritus of Bellevue Baptist Church in Memphis, Tennessee. Dr. Lee concluded the meeting he held at First Baptist with his famous sermon, "Payday Someday," delivered to an overflow crowd estimated at 1,400 people. In addition to revivals and Bible studies, Graves' evangelistic focus included spreading the gospel through mission trips to the Rio Grande Valley and choir tours. To facilitate these efforts and to provide transportation for senior adult trips and taking youth groups to camp, the congregation purchased the first of a series of four buses owned by First Baptist, a used Continental Trailways diesel. Repainted in SFA colors of purple and white, the bus was dubbed "The Purple Goose" by members of the congregation.

Since Jared Cartlidge's second pastorate, First Baptist Sunday morning services had been broadcast over radio stations KSFA and KOSF, which became KEEE. In March 1971, Graves recommended televising the morning worship service over the local television cable for a three-month trial period. In August the congregation approved a two-month extension of the television broadcast. Although it did not continue, this effort established a precedent for the congregation's present television ministry.

"IN 1966 WE MOVED TO NACOGDOCHES AND PURCHASED THE ONLY HOUSE FOR SALE . . . A SMALL HOME ON PEARL [STREET] NEXT DOOR TO MILDRED AND BEE SITTON. MILDRED BECAME MY PRINCIPAL AND VERY CLOSE FRIEND AND ADVISOR. ONE DAY DR. EDWIN CRAWFORD, NOT GETTING AN ANSWER AT OUR FRONT DOOR, WALKED AROUND TO THE BACK ONLY TO BE GREETED BY A HASTILY CONSTRUCTED WIRE FENCE FOR THE DOG OF THE FAMILY. HE QUICKLY CLIMBED OVER THE FENCE, GRABBED CHARLES' HAND, AND WELCOMED US TO NACOGDOCHES. I TOLD DR. CRAWFORD THAT WE HAD EVERY INTENTION OF JOINING FIRST BAPTIST CHURCH BECAUSE MY FATHER WAS A MINISTER AND ONLY OF *FIRST* BAPTIST CHURCHES!"
Mary Neal Grimland

On Sunday, December 5, 1971, Graves resigned as pastor of First Baptist to return to Bangor, Maine, as an evangelist and Christian motivational speaker. His wife and daughter returned to Bangor with him, but Graves' two sons, Gordon and Keith, and their wives remained in East Texas. In 1972, the Columbia Street Baptist Church in Bangor called him to serve a second time as its pastor. He accepted and continued in this position until his death July 30, 1975. After his death, Graves' wife, Shirley, returned to Nacogdoches to be closer to her children and grandchildren.

Two months after Graves' resignation, the church elected a pulpit committee to find a new pastor. The committee, chaired by John O. Sutton, lost no time in getting to work. By April 3, the committee recommended that Bill R. Austin, pastor of Calvary Baptist Church in Waco, Texas, be invited to preach in view of a call on Sunday, April 9. After meeting Austin and hearing him preach, the congregation agreed that he should be the church's twentieth pastor. He accepted, and the church held a service of consecration for their new pastor on April 26, 1972. Former First Baptist pastor, Edwin Crawford, the local superintendent of missions for the Waco area, wrote his former congregation praising Austin and expressing a sense of loss for his leaving Waco.

Austin attended public school in Abilene, Texas, earned a bachelor's degree from Hardin-Simmons University in Abilene, and attended Southwestern Baptist Theological Seminary in Fort Worth, Texas. He earned his master of arts and doctor of philosophy degrees from Baylor University in Waco, Texas. When called by First Baptist, Austin had not completed his doctorate, but the church allowed him to take time to finish it while he served as pastor. In addition to Calvary Baptist Church, Austin pastored the First Baptist Church of Waxahachie, Texas, and the First Baptist Church of Vernon, Texas, before coming to Nacogdoches.

When Austin arrived in Nacogdoches with his wife, Margie, and their daughter Terri—son Randy was attending his first year of college at Baylor University—he found a congregation he characterized as "expectant and responsive" to his leadership as pastor.[10] During his tenure the congregation experienced growth, especially in the number of SFA students who became members or participated in programs such as the university choir led by minister of music Larry McFadden. Austin's wife, Margie, taught the young married couples Sunday school class. When she began, the class

A NEW DAY AT FIRST BAPTIST CHURCH
411 NORTH STREET
Lionel Crowell, PASTOR

One of the first tasks facing Lionel Crowell after he assumed the pastorate of First Baptist was the assembling of a staff. By the fall of 1975, he had a staff in place and could advertise that there was a new day at First Baptist Church. Shown are Crowell, minister of education Ken Etley, minister of music Bruce Swihart, and minister of youth and recreation Wes Skeeters. *Nacogdoches Daily Sentinel.*

had seventeen members. When Austin's tenure came to a close, the class had grown to eighty-seven members.

Austin strongly promoted tithing. Church finances improved, and giving exceeded the budget. The church's gifts to the Southern Baptist Convention's Cooperative Program, associational missions, the Baptist Student Union, and special mission offerings increased to the point where the congregation's giving to mission causes outside the local church equaled 25 percent of its income. The improvement in finances allowed the church to begin planning for future expansion of its facilities and to budget funds for an activities director. Twelve thousand dollars from the budget in 1973 and another $12,000 from the budget in 1974 were designated to begin a building fund. An Activities Building Ideas Committee was appointed to develop plans for a family life center to meet the recreational and fellowship needs of the congregation and provide an outreach to the community. Before plans for the activities building were completed, Austin resigned to accept a call to University Baptist Church in Abilene, Texas. He characterized his two-year pastorate in Nacogdoches as "short, but sweet."[11] When he left, the pulpit committee that brought him to First Baptist gave him a surprise dinner party. Years later, Austin commented that no other church had ever done that. At the time of his resignation in February 1974, Austin's daughter, Terri, was only a few months away from completing her senior year of high school, so the church allowed her mother and her to continue to live in the parsonage until after she was graduated.

Following his pastorate of University Baptist Church, Austin served as pastor of First Baptist Church of Ponca City, Oklahoma, and Elkins

"THIS HUGE STEP OF FAITH [THE BUILDING OF THE CHRISTIAN LIFE CENTER] HAS BEEN A MARVELOUS BLESSING FOR EXTENDING OUR CHURCH OUTREACH IN A WAY THAT WE NEVER DREAMED POSSIBLE. IT LAID THE FOUNDATION FOR OUR WILLINGNESS TO TAKE ANOTHER GIANT STEP OF FAITH WHEN WE AGREED TO BUILD THE CHILDREN'S BUILDING."

Dr. Doyle Alexander, Chairman of the CLC Building Committee

Lake Baptist Church in Huntsville, Texas. In addition he served on the faculties of Hardin-Simmons University in Abilene, Texas, and Temple College in Temple, Texas, as chaplain of Baylor University, and as interim pastor of several churches. Austin is the author of twelve books and numerous articles. He has served on the executive board of the Baptist General Convention of Texas, on several Baptist General Convention of Texas commissions and committees, and as trustee of Hardin-Simmons University and Hillcrest Baptist Medical Center. In 1984, Austin returned to preach at First Baptist as part of the church's celebration of its one-hundredth anniversary. Since March 1, 2008, he has been pastor of Park Lake Drive Baptist Church in Waco, Texas.

Following Austin's resignation, First Baptist once again was in need of a pastor. This time, the pastoral supply committee recommended employing an interim pastor while the new pulpit committee conducted its search. Dr. Billy Simmons, professor of religion and chair of the Department of Religion of East Texas Baptist College in Marshall, Texas, was chosen as interim pastor. He served in this position until the pulpit committee, chaired by L. D. Pate, brought a recommendation for the Reverend Paul Lionel Crowell, pastor of the First Baptist Church in Leesville, Louisiana, to preach in view of a call on October 13, 1974. For the first time, a pulpit committee of the church included two student members, Sherrie Sweat and Kerry Horn. Half the committee heard Crowell preach in his Leesville church on August 25 and were so impressed that the other half traveled to Leesville to hear him preach on September 1. The entire committee was impressed with Crowell's pastoral and administrative skills, his experience with building programs, and the length of tenure of his last two pastorates, eleven and five years, respectively. In addition, Simmons, the church's interim pastor, had attended New Orleans Baptist Theological Seminary with Crowell and gave him a strong endorsement.

On October 13, the Sunday morning that he was to preach in view of a call, Crowell, his wife, Mary Alice, and their two daughters, Deborah (Debbie) and Lola, were at the Fredonia Hotel dressing to go to the Sunday morning service when he bent over to tie his shoes and experienced severe back spasms. He lay down thinking the pain would get better, but it persisted. When he stood up, it was so intense he fainted and fell across the bed. When his wife told L. D. Pate, the chairman of the pulpit committee, that her husband would not be able to preach, Pate thought she was teasing. When she convinced him it was true, he immediately called a doctor to attend Crowell in the hotel. George Loutherback, the Stephen F. Austin Baptist Student Union director, was called to fill the pulpit, and the afternoon reception for the Crowell family was cancelled. Crowell remained at the hotel in bed for three days. When he returned to Leesville, a lady in

During Lionel Crowell's pastorate, First Baptist celebrated its long history with "Old Fashioned" Sundays. Church members dressed in the fashions of past eras and enjoyed "dinner on the grounds" after the morning worship service.

Left: Bennett and Ruth Cooksey. *Courtesy of Ruth Cooksey.*

Right: Jeramy Prince, Jerry Prince, Melanie Goodson, and Jackie Prince. *First Baptist Church Archives.*

his church there told him she felt terrible because she had prayed that he would not be able to get up and preach in Nacogdoches and she feared her prayer was the cause of his problem. Two weeks later, Crowell returned to Nacogdoches and preached. The congregation extended him a call, and by Thanksgiving he had moved his family to Nacogdoches.

Prior to extending a call to Crowell, the congregation discussed selling the parsonage and providing a housing allowance for future pastors. In discussions with prospective pastors, the pulpit committee discovered that many, including Crowell, preferred for the church to provide a housing allowance instead of a parsonage. Providing a housing allowance, they said, was becoming a trend and enabled ministers to accumulate equity so that they could purchase a home of their own at retirement. The parsonage was sold, and since that time First Baptist has paid its pastors a housing allowance in lieu of providing them a parsonage.

Crowell was graduated from Ouachita High School in Monroe, from Louisiana College in Pineville, and from New Orleans Baptist Seminary in New Orleans, all in Louisiana. Prior to First Baptist, all of his pastorates were in Louisiana, where he served on various committees and boards of the local Baptist associations, the Louisiana Baptist Convention, and the Southern Baptist Convention. He was president of the alumni association of Louisiana Baptist Theological Seminary and a trustee of Louisiana College. Crowell also was actively involved in community affairs. He served on the board of Leesville-Vernon Parish Chamber of Commerce and chaired the Vernon Parish United Fund. He continued to be involved in denominational and civic affairs after arriving in Nacogdoches, serving

The Blue Goose
and Its Successors

In the fall of 1969, the Reverend Bob Graves led First Baptist to purchase a used Continental Trailways motor coach. The bus, Graves said, "will be a great boost to our senior citizens ministry and our youth program. It will enable all our choirs to participate in state festivals. We will be able to make choir tours and a couple of trips each year to Glorieta."[1] The newly acquired bus was painted in SFA colors, but when the paint turned out to be more blue than purple, it was affectionately (or maybe not so affectionately) dubbed "The Blue Goose" by members of the congregation. The First Baptist Church youth and senior citizens, as well as The Sound Generation, the university choir led by First Baptist Church music minister Earl Davis, used it extensively for trips. The bus was already well used when acquired by the church. After a few years, it began to need more and more repairs, so a new Thomas-built air-conditioned school bus was purchased as a replacement. The Thomas bus served well for a time, but as the miles began to pile up, it, too, had a tendency to break down on trips and leave groups stranded by the roadside. After returning from one such trip in August 1984, one of the deacons, Myrten Doss, gave $1,000 to start a fund for a new bus. By October 1986, the fund had grown enough that a used Silver Eagle coach could be purchased for $119,500. It served the congregation's needs until replacement parts began to be difficult to obtain and a new, forty-five-foot Le Mirage XLZ coach was purchased as a replacement in April 2000. Owning a bus has enabled many First Baptist groups to go on mission trips and choir tours, attend camps and retreats, and travel in the company of Christian friends and church members.

First Baptist Church's first bus, the Blue Goose. *First Baptist Church Archives.*

---

1. Bob Graves, Pastor's Paragraphs, *The Baptist Standard, First Baptist Church, Nacogdoches Edition,* November 5, 1969.

"I REMEMBER ALL OF THE
DIFFERENT BUSES THAT
WE'VE HAD—FROM THE
"PURPLE GOOSE" WITH JIM
METZGER DRIVING, THE
OLD SCHOOL BUS WITH WES
SKEETERS DRIVING AND
"HAULING" KIDS ON MIS-
SION TRIPS, AND THEN AD-
VANCING TO THE TRAILWAYS
BUS WITH DAVID CAMPBELL
DRIVING AND TAKING THE
SENIOR ADULTS TO THE
EAST COAST. THE CHURCH
BUS TODAY IS THE CADILLAC
OF ALL THE BUSES THAT WE
HAVE HAD. THERE HAVE
BEEN MANY GOOD TIMES AND
GOOD TRIPS WITH BOBBY
SMITH, BRAD HAILE, AND
ROCKY JOHNSON."

Ann Sweat

Top: The air-conditioned Thomas-built school bus purchased new by First Baptist Church. *First Baptist Church Archives.*

Center: First Baptist Church's used Silver Eagle bus at the George Bush Presidential Library and Museum in 1999. *First Baptist Church Archives.*

Bottom: The new 2000 Le Mirage XLZ coach ready to leave for Hodges Gardens, Louisiana—spring 2008. *Photo by Brenda Howard.*

as trustee of East Texas Baptist University, president of the Nacogdoches Ministerial Alliance, and moderator of the East Texas Area Baptist Association. He was also a member of the Nacogdoches Rotary Club and on the board of the Nacogdoches United Way.

Crowell's wife, Mary Alice, in addition to teaching Sunday school and many other activities of a pastor's wife, worked as a graduate assistant in the Stephen F. Austin's Department of Business with First Baptist members Jean Rudisill and Carolyn Price while completing her master's degree. Afterwards, she joined the faculty of Nacogdoches High School, teaching business subjects.

When he arrived in Nacogdoches, Crowell continued the planning for an activities building that had begun under Austin. In April 1975, the congregation elected a Long Range Planning Committee, chaired by Jimmy Partin, and charged it with investigating the future needs of the church, including a possible facility for recreational and other church-related activities. The committee submitted its recommendations to the church in January 1976. They included renovation and remodeling of the existing facilities plus constructing an activities building. Two committees, a Building Construction Committee, chaired by Doyle Alexander, and a Building Finance Committee, chaired by Bill McWhorter, were elected in February to begin planning. By September the church had employed Don Tew, an Austin architect, to work with the Building Construction Committee to develop plans for the new facility.

In February 1977, the church approved Tew's plans and the Building Finance Committee began soliciting pledges to raise one-third of the estimated construction cost. Resource Services Inc. was employed to guide the fund-raising campaign titled "Together We Grow." The campaign secured pledges of $450,000 to be paid over a three-year period. Bids on the new building were solicited, and church member Tom Evans of T. G. Evans Construction Company won the bid. Financing was secured from Texas Commerce Bank in Houston, Texas, and on a cold, windy Sunday in January 1978, the congregation gathered at the rear of the church to break ground for the new facility. At a total cost of over $1.5 million and almost 35,000 square feet, the project was the most ambitious building project the congregation had undertaken. After two years of construction, during which Evans worked tirelessly to complete the project within the budget, the facility was finished. On Sunday, January 27, 1980, the congregation joined in vows to "consecrate ourselves anew and dedicate this building to the teaching and living of the whole gospel of our Lord and Savior, Jesus Christ."[12]

The new Christian Life Building included facilities for a wide variety of recreational and craft activities as well as a remodeled and expanded kitchen, a music suite, and educational space. The new Preschool Building provided space for the care of infants and young children during church services and activities, as well as the church's Day School for three-, four-, and five-year-olds. Before the Preschool Building was constructed, some of the Day School classes met on the second floor of the south wing, requiring the children to pass the pastor's study. Crowell recalls that the teachers would caution the children to be quiet because the pastor was studying. One of the teachers reported to him that one day as they passed the study, a little boy told the other children, "Quiet, the Holy Ghost lives in there!"[13]

The space vacated in the south wing by relocating the nursery and preschool children's programs to the new building was remodeled into a reception area and office suite. For the first time, staff members, who had been scattered all over the building, were located in the same area. Additional space was also provided for an expanded library, and improvements were made to the heating and cooling systems.

With the new Christian Life Center completed, First Baptist launched a full program of activities for children, youth, and adults planned by Wes Skeeters, the youth and activities director. There were bowling leagues, aerobics groups, skating nights, basketball teams, racquetball tournaments, and family night movies with popcorn and soft drinks. Classes were offered in ceramics, watercolor painting, photography, stained glass, needlepoint, and a variety of other crafts and special interests. Church members and their families brought friends and guests as an outreach into the community and for Christian fellowship. For many members of the congregation, and especially teenagers and university students, the church became the center of their social activities as well as their spiritual home.

"GETTING THE MONEY TO BUILD THE CLC AND REMODEL THE FACILITIES WAS QUITE AN UNDERTAKING. AT FIRST IT ACTUALLY LOOKED IMPOSSIBLE. THE BUDGET AND FINANCE COMMITTEE HAD PREPARED ABOUT A DOZEN LOAN PACKAGES AND NO REPLY HAD BEEN RECEIVED . . . TIME WAS RUNNING OUT BECAUSE OF THE CONTRACT DEADLINE. IT JUST SEEMED LIKE THINGS WERE NOT WORKING OUT. ONE DAY I RETURNED TO MY OFFICE VERY DEPRESSED. I BOWED MY HEAD ON MY DESK AND JUST PRAYED FOR THE LORD TO GIVE GUIDANCE AND DIRECTION. IN ABOUT TEN MINUTES THE PHONE RANG. IT WAS A LOCAL BANKER. HE ASKED ME TO BRING THE PACKAGE TO HIS OFFICE AND TALK TO HIM ABOUT IT. HIS FATHER WAS THE TREASURER OF A BAPTIST CHURCH, SO HE KNEW THE MECHANICS AND FINANCES OF BAPTIST CHURCHES. HE CALLED THE VICE PRESIDENT OF TEXAS COMMERCE BANK IN HOUSTON AND ASKED HIM TO LOOK OVER THE PACKAGE. THE HOUSTON BANKER SAID THAT THE LAST LOAN MEETING OF THE YEAR WOULD BE THE NEXT DAY AT 9:00 A.M. BECAUSE THE NEXT WEEK WAS CHRISTMAS. IT WAS 3:00 P.M. THEN. I WENT HOME, THREW SOME THINGS IN A SUITCASE AND LEFT FOR HOUSTON. I WENT TO THE MAN'S HOUSE IN HOUSTON, AND WE LOOKED AT THE PACKAGE UNTIL MIDNIGHT. THE NEXT MORNING WE GOT UP AT 4:00 A.M. AND WENT DOWNTOWN TO THE BANK. HE TOOK SEVERAL LOAN PACKAGES INTO THE COMMITTEE MEETING. WITHIN A SHORT TIME HE CAME OUT AND HANDED ME A LETTER APPROVING A LOAN FOR $1,670,000. I CAME BACK TO NACOGDOCHES KNOWING THAT THE LORD HAD WORKED THIS OUT AND WE COULD GO ON WITH OUR PROJECT."

Bill McWhorter

On a cold, windy January day in 1978, the most senior members of the congregation broke ground for the Christian Life Center, the first new construction by First Baptist in three decades. Left to right are Ina Eddings, Ross Fountain, Grace Monk, Agnes Rogers, and Maggie Gallaway. *First Baptist Church Archives.*

The Long Range Planning Committee also recommended that First Baptist continue to purchase property adjacent to the church whenever it became available. During this period the Branch-Patton and Arch Price properties, as well as a filling station located south of the church, were purchased to provide for future expansion. While the Christian Life Center was under construction, the Branch-Patton building was used for church activities. After the Christian Life Center was completed in 1980, the building and the service station were demolished to enable expansion of the south parking lot.

Ministering to university students remained a priority of First Baptist. Members of the congregation "adopted" students who joined the church, inviting them into their homes and including them in family activities. This Adopt-A-Student program led to many students forming close relationships with First Baptist families that lasted long after their college days. There were other results from the student ministry as well. When a major flood of Nacogdoches' two creeks occurred in 1975, Crowell received a telephone call from a mother in Louisiana asking him to check on her daughter and son-in-law who were students at Stephen F. Austin. Crowell braved the flood to find them and report that they were safe. The two joined First Baptist, and later, when Crowell was visiting the First Baptist Church in Monroe, Louisiana, the pastor called on him to pray and told the story of how Crowell had come to check on him and his wife during the flood. As Crowell observed, "Interest in and caring for people has its rewards."[14]

The Christian Life Center was built immediately west of and connected to the north wing of the church plant. Don Tew of Austin was the architect, and Evans Construction of Nacogdoches was the contractor. *First Baptist Church Archives.*

Skating in the gym

The new Christian Life Center provided a place for the church family and guests to enjoy recreation and fellowship. The gymnasium provided space for basketball, games, and skating as well as that most favorite of all Baptist pastimes—eating. The lower floor housed a bowling alley and racquetball court. Classrooms provided space for hobby classes such as ceramics, and the second floor contained Sunday school rooms and rehearsal and dressing space for the music program. *First Baptist Church Archives.*

Games in the gym

Bowling

Banquet in the gym

Ceramics Room

Choir Rehearsal Room—Dick Branson and Youth Choir

The Senior Adult Sunday School Department meets in the lower auditorium of the main church building. This photograph shows the members of the department during Lionel Crowell's pastorate. *First Baptist Church Archives.*

Crowell encouraged members of the congregation to lead an evangelistic lifestyle and promoted a Lay Renewal Weekend designed to help church members renew their Christian walk and their commitment to witnessing. A series of Christian Growth Adventure Revivals were conducted by laymen of the church and held in small Baptist churches throughout East Texas. In 1979, thirteen Five Day Clubs were led in their neighborhoods by forty-four women of the congregation, resulting in the conversion of thirty children, and three WIN Schools were conducted to instruct members in how to witness to others.

Before construction of the Children's Building, the first grade children's Sunday school met on the second floor of the south wing. Teachers shown, left to right, are Jane Chambers (standing), L. D. Pate, Ron Canfield, and Lila Moorer (seated). *First Baptist Church Archives.*

On May 25, 1980, four months after the dedication of the Christian Life Center, Crowell resigned from First Baptist to accept a call from the Emanuel Baptist Church of Alexandria, Louisiana, effective June 22. In leaving he expressed puzzlement over why he should feel the Lord leading him to another church when First Baptist was growing and experiencing success in so many areas, and he thanked the congregation for the love they extended to him and his family. Crowell served as pastor of Emanuel Baptist until 1983, when he left to become the pastor of Ridge Avenue Baptist Church of West Monroe, Louisiana, the church where he was baptized as a child. On January 1, 1998, he retired from Ridge Avenue Baptist but not from the ministry. He served successively as pastor of Kitzingen Baptist Church of Kitzingen, Germany; chaplain of Glenwood Regional Medical Center in West Monroe, Louisiana; interim pastor of First Baptist Church, Vienna, Louisiana; and interim pastor of Kitzingen Baptist Church of Kitzingen, Germany. He and his wife, Mary Alice, reside in West Monroe, Louisiana. He continues to accept preaching engagements, and he and his wife enjoy being grandparents to seven grandchildren. When they reflect on their time at First Baptist in Nacogdoches, they recall the congregation as "great, gracious church family filled with wonderful people" where they saw God's power at work many times.[15]

---

1. Unidentified, undated newspaper clipping in First Baptist Church scrapbook.

2. Interview of W. Edwin Crawford with Rose Ann Pool, August 13, 1983.

3. Ibid.

4. Interview of Johnny Rudisill Jr. with Jean Rudisill, April 8, 2008.

5. *Baptist Standard, First Baptist Church Nacogdoches Edition*, June 7, 1967.

6. W. Edwin Crawford, "Pastor Announces His Resignation," *Baptist Standard, First Baptist Church Nacogdoches Edition*, May 17, 1967.

7. Southwestern Baptist Theological Seminary *Newsletter*, November 1983.

8. E-mail Dan Crawford to Jean Rudisill, June 7, 2008.

9. Rick Scarborough, "About Us," Vision American Homepage, http://www.visionamerica.us.

10. Bill R. Austin, "Pastor Resigns to Accept Abilene Church," *Baptist Standard, First Baptist Church, Nacogdoches Edition*, February 20, 1974.

11. Bill Austin to Jean Rudisill, 2008.

12. Program of Dedication Services of the Christian Life Center, Preschool Building, and Modernized Facilities, January 27, 1980, First Baptist Church archives.

13. Lionel and Mary Alice Crowell, "Memories at First Baptist Nacogdoches," MS given to Jean Rudisill, 2008.

14. Ibid.

15. Ibid.

"IN 1974, WHEN I WAS SEVEN YEARS OLD, THE SANCTUARY WAS BEING RENOVATED AND SO CHURCH SERVICES WERE HELD IN THE GYM OF THE CHRISTIAN LIFE CENTER. I REMEMBER WALKING DOWN THE AISLE OF THE GYM TO PROFESS MY FAITH. I WAS BAPTIZED IN LINDA CLIFTON'S SWIMMING POOL, ALONG WITH A FEW OTHER CHILDREN [BECAUSE THE BAPTISTRY WAS UNUSABLE DURING THE RENOVATIONS]."

Jenny (Harris) Lewallen

6

Building the Church

*"It remains to this day the 'best of things'
to give oneself to building the church."*

Wayne Dehoney
Set the Church Afire

As the summer of 1980 began, First Baptist Church was once more in need of a pastor. A search committee was elected and immediately began looking for a minister to replace Dr. Lionel Crowell. In the meantime, Dr. Donald Potts, chairman of the Department of Religion at East Texas Baptist College in Marshall, Texas, served as interim pastor and conducted the weekly services.

When Dr. George Thompson, chairman of the pastor search committee, announced to the congregation that the committee had invited a young Baptist minister from Quitman, Texas, to preach in view of a call on February 1, 1981, he said they did so "with much pleasure and excitement."[1] That minister was Dr. Allen Reed, who became the twenty-second individual to pastor the First Baptist Church of Nacogdoches. His twenty-eight-year pastorate is the longest in the congregation's history and is almost twice that of the church's second-longest tenured pastor, Bonnie Grimes.

The day Reed preached dawned grey and cloudy, a typical February day in East Texas. As he stood to speak, the sun broke through the clouds

Opposite: Dr. Allen Reed is known and loved for his Bible-based expository preaching delivered faithfully each Sunday. Casual dress is the rule at First Baptist Church for the hot summer months. *Photo by Jimmy Partin.*

The Reverend Reed's family early in his ministry at First Baptist Church, left to right, are Carrie, Micah, Linda, David, and Allen Reed. *First Baptist Church Archives.*

and a ray of sunlight beamed through the stained glass windows of the auditorium and shone on the pulpit. One member of the congregation later remarked that it was not the "sunshine [on the pulpit] that impressed the congregation, it was the 'Sonshine' [the congregation] felt" from the pulpit that led them to issue a call for Reed to pastor the church.[2]

Charles Allen Reed is a native East Texan. He was born October 13, 1943, in Pittsburg, Texas, the youngest of four sons born to Orvel Herschel Reed and Lizzie Mae (Fowler) Reed. He grew up in Pittsburg, attended Pittsburg public schools, and graduated from Pittsburg High School in 1962. In his personal testimony, Reed related that in the summer of 1952, when he was nine years old, he and his older brother Gerald began asking questions about becoming Christians. Their father took them on a Sunday afternoon to visit their pastor, the Reverend Eugene Moore, who explained the plan of salvation to them. "There was nothing dramatic about my conversion experience," Reed said, "but I believe it was genuine. I made my decision public that same evening at the evening worship service and was baptized shortly thereafter."[3]

When Reed was a seventeen-year-old high school junior, he began to feel a call to preach. Three men he respected, E. S. Shirley, his pastor at that time, Bill Beckham, a seminary student from his church, and the Reverend E. P. Wooten, his next-door neighbor and employer, were instrumental in his decision to enter the ministry. "I have never doubted my call into the ministry," Reed stated. "I am more convinced each day that I am in the center of God's will for my life. God opened up many opportunities for me to preach almost immediately, and I've been preaching ever since."[4] Reed preached his first sermon from notes written on two index cards the Sunday following his public decision to enter the ministry. On May 21,

Convinced that the Lord had led them to a "keeper," the pulpit committee that recommended the church call Allen Reed as pastor organized themselves into the "Finders, Keepers Club" and met occasionally to celebrate their "find." Members and their spouses were, left to right, John Sutton, Beverly Sutton, Lila Moorer, Milton Moorer, Bill Sylvester, Carolyn Sylvester, Jewel Akridge, Caroline Thompson, Ruth Cooksey, Johnny Rudisill, Jean Rudisill, Linda Reed, and Allen Reed. Members of the committee not pictured are Don Prince, Charles Pool, and committee chairman, George Thompson. *Photo courtesy of Allen Reed.*

In 1992 First Baptist Church celebrated paying off the loan for construction of the Christian Life Center, Preschool Building, and office renovations by burning the note in the Sunday morning worship service. Dr. Lionel Crowell (right), pastor when the construction took place, returned to participate as Dr. Allen Reed (left) lit the note held by Bill McWhorter (center), who chaired the Building Finance Committee for the project. *First Baptist Church Archives.*

1961, while he was still in high school, his home church, the First Baptist Church of Pittsburg, Texas, licensed him to preach. Later, on June 5, 1965, the church ordained Reed to the gospel ministry.

After graduating from high school, Reed attended East Texas Baptist College in Marshall, Texas, where he met and married Linda Gail Vanderburg, the daughter of S. C. (Sam) and Leatha Vanderburg, of Conroe, Texas. For two summers while in college, Reed served as youth director in Baptist churches. He was youth director in his home church in Pittsburg, Texas, in the summer of 1963, and youth director in the First Baptist Church of Vidor, Texas, in the summer of 1964. One year after his marriage, Reed graduated from East Texas Baptist College with a BA degree in sociology and speech. He immediately enrolled in Southwestern Baptist Theological Seminary in Fort Worth, Texas, where he earned a Master of Divinity degree in 1969. Like many seminary students, Reed pastored churches while attending school. From 1964 to 1968, he was pastor of Midway Baptist Church in Gilmer, Texas. In 1968, he was called to the First Baptist Church of Cumby, Texas, where he served until 1971, when he moved to Gateway Baptist Church (formerly Braeburn Glen Baptist Church), in Dallas, Texas. In 1975, Reed answered a call to the First Baptist Church of Quitman, Texas, where he served until coming to Nacogdoches. During his early pastorates, he continued his studies at Southwestern Baptist Theological Seminary and earned the degree of Doctor of Ministry in 1980.

Reed's wife, Linda, is an active pastor's wife and helpmate. She put her degree in business education from East Texas Baptist College to use as a high school business teacher, as a teacher of preschool children in the First

One of the first ministerial staff members selected by Reed was Bobby Smith, shown with wife Laura. The church called Smith as minister of youth and activities on April 1, 1983. In 2009, Smith served the congregation as associate pastor and minister to university students. *First Baptist Church Archives.*

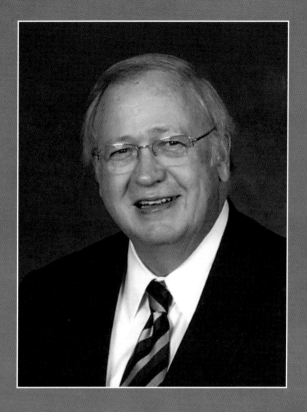

"DR. REED HAS ALWAYS
TAKEN THE TIME TO LISTEN
AND HELP ONE IN NEED.
HIS HONESTY, INTEGRITY,
AND ABILITY TO BE A GOOD
LISTENER ARE APPRECIATED
VERY MUCH. AFTER THE
DEATH OF MY HUSBAND, WHAT
MEANT SO MUCH TO ME WAS
NOT ONLY THE EXCELLENT
SPIRITUAL COUNSELING I
RECEIVED, BUT [ALSO] THE
PERSONAL CONCERN AND TIME
HE TOOK WITH ME."

Ruth Cooksey

Dr. Charles Allen Reed

Allen Reed is the twenty-second individual to pastor First Baptist
Church and is the longest tenured of the congregation's pastors.
He began his ministry at First Baptist Church on March 1, 1981.
His service as pastor of the church has been marked by his Bible-
based preaching, his love for the members of his congregation, and
his strong sense of humor. At the banquet celebrating the 125th
anniversary of the establishment of First Baptist Church, Ed Pool,
a third-generation member of the congregation, paid the following
tribute to Reed. "In your twenty-eight years as our beloved pastor,
you have . . . touched each of us in many ways. You have baptized
our children, performed our weddings, buried our loved ones, walked
with us, and have given us a hand of encouragement and friend-
ship. But, above all, you have loved us with a Christ-like heart. Your
loyalty and devotion, first to our Lord and then to the congregation,
has been a gracious gift, given freely from a heart filled with God's
unspeakable love." *Photo courtesy of Allen Reed.*

Baptist Day School, and in the office of Nacogdoches High School. She is a talented musician, and, in addition to her involvement in many church ministries, she has served as the church organist for twenty-five years. The Reeds are the parents of three children, David Allen Reed, now serving as Minister of Youth for his father's congregation at First Baptist Church, Micah Scott Reed, who resides with his family in Fort Worth, Texas, and Carrie Elizabeth (Reed) Blumhoff, of Daphne, Alabama. The Reeds are grandparents to six grandchildren.

Reed preached his first sermon as pastor of First Baptist Church on Sunday, March 1, 1981. In the message he delivered that Sunday, Reed committed himself to building the church and outlined seven criteria for a great church. It must be, he said, a Christ-centered, redeemed, Bible-believing, soul-winning, mission-minded, Holy Spirit–filled, active, and growing congregation. In the years that followed, these criteria have been the common threads of continuity in every aspect of his ministry of building the body of believers known as First Baptist Church.[5] When Reed arrived at his office the following Monday morning, he was greeted by the small church staff of Wes Skeeters, minister of youth and recreation, Jim Jenkins, interim minister of music, Mary Cunningham, church secretary and receptionist, Patsy Sullivan, part-time financial secretary, Allison Maricle, Christian Life Center secretary, and Joe Jones, building superintendent. "Mr. Joe" took the new pastor on a tour of the building, including what he referred to as "The Pastors' Picture Hall,"

The First Baptist ministerial staff in 1989 included (front row seated, left to right) Jim McDonald, minister of education & administration, and Allen Reed, pastor. Second row (standing, left to right): Bobby Smith, minister of youth; Dwight Evans, minister of recreation; Mark Price, minister to adults; and David Campbell, minister of music. *First Baptist Church Archives.*

Rain or shine, hot or cold, members of the Greeters Ministry make First Baptist Church guests and members feel welcome. Ned and Donna Fowler (left) are greeted by Cheryl and Robert VanNorman. *Photo by Jimmy Partin.*

Linda Reed, church organist and the pastor's wife. *Photo by Tom Atchison.*

Richard Chambers, church pianist. *Photo by Jimmy Partin.*

Linda Reed on the organ and Richard Chambers on the piano accompany the Celebration Choir and other singing groups each Sunday. Reed has served as the church organist for twenty-five years.

The members of the church orchestra provide an additional musical dimension to weekly worship services and special presentations. *Photo by Jimmy Partin.*

Beginning in the 1940s, First Baptist Church broadcast its Sunday morning worship services over local radio stations. In 2009, services are recorded and telecast over station KTRE TV. Recordings and videos of the services are available for church members who are shut-in or who want to have a recording of a special service. *Photo by Jimmy Partin.*

The Celebration Choir, led by minister of music Andre Simon, establishes an atmosphere of worship every Sunday morning. *Photo by Jimmy Partin.*

The Hand Bell Choir performed in the Gift of Christmas program of December 2008, continuing a tradition begun when the Bunkie Reid family donated a set of hand bells to the church during the Reverend Edwin Crawford's pastorate. *Photo by Jimmy Partin.*

In observing the Ordinance of Baptism, Dr. Allen Reed always asks the candidates if they believe Jesus Christ is the Son of God and if they have trusted him as their Savior. Following their public testimony, he immerses them in the baptismal waters. *First Baptist Church Archives.*

First Baptist Church children combine music and drama to present Biblical truth. The summer musical in 2008, *Hans Bronson's Gold Medal*, had an Olympic theme and taught the children that spiritual strength is as important as physical strength. Children's music leader Marcy Davis directed the summer musical.

Top: Children's music leader Marcy Davis. *Photo by Paul Cook.*

Bottom: Children performing in the summer musical in 2008. *Photo by Paul Cook.*

where he urged Reed to get his picture made quickly since, as "Mr. Joe" stated, "Don't none of 'em stay very long." As time would prove, Allen Reed became the exception to relatively short-term pastorates at First Baptist.[6] During his tenure as pastor of First Baptist Church, the congregation has experienced growth in membership and giving, improved and added to the church facilities, acquired additional property for future expansion, expanded existing ministries and established new ministries, sponsored new Baptist churches, and increased its participation in both North American and international missions.

Among the initial challenges Reed faced as the church's new pastor was increasing the staff to better meet the needs of the congregation. Convinced that he could do a better job of preparing sermons and ministering to the congregation if there was another minister to attend to the day-to-day business of church operations, Reed called on Jim McDonald, a friend from college days, to serve as the administrator of the business and educational functions of the church. In 1982, Jeff Blevins was added as minister of music, and the church approved dividing the responsibilities for youth and recreation into two positions and added the position of minister to university students. Bobby Smith was called as youth minister, Steve Lemmond as recreation minister, and Mark Price was hired as the congregation's first minister to university students. Adding these positions expanded the number of ministerial staff to six, where it remained until the position of children's minister was created in 1997.

With a staff in place, Reed turned his attention to other needs of the church and published a list of fourteen objectives that he asked the congregation to address. These objectives included reaching the lost and unchurched people of the community, providing strong educational and youth programs, emphasizing missions, increasing the church's ministry to university students, emphasizing stewardship, and improving media outreach through radio broadcasts of services, a tape ministry, and a newspaper column. By 1986, as the congregation prepared to celebrate Reed's fifth anniversary as the church's pastor and his twenty-fifth year in the ministry, it was evident that progress had been made on almost all of these objectives. A full staff was in place. Sunday services were broadcast on the radio, and Reed was writing a weekly column, "Reed All About It," for the *Daily Sentinel*. Sunday school enrollment and average attendance had

Banner Ministry

Romans 8:28 states, "And we know that in all things God works for the good of those who love him…" NIV. That is exactly what happened one Sunday morning when Barbara Harris was at home with the flu and watched the services of Bellevue Baptist Church in Memphis, Tennessee, on television. The program featured the church's banner ministry. When Harris saw the banners presented, she knew that creating beautiful banners could be an exciting ministry for First Baptist, and she shared her impression with Rose Ann Pool. Together they solicited the support of Dr. Reed and David Campbell, the minister of music, for recruiting church members interested in fabrics and sewing in a banner ministry. From the beginning the banners focused on depicting the names of the Savior. Each woman participating in the ministry engaged in personal Bible study and prayed for revelation of the name to use in designing her banner. The first banner completed was "Mighty Warrior." By the end of the ministry's first year, four or five banners had been sewn. There are now thirty-six completed banners, each focusing on one Biblical name for Jesus Christ. All are original designs, and each creator of a banner shared how the design was revealed to her, why she chose each color, and the symbolism involved in the design.

Early in their work, the banner creators realized that although they had designed and made the banners, they did not own them—they belonged to the Lord, to be used how and when He should lead. The first presentation using the banners was *Blessed Be The Names* on April 8, 1990. The banners have been used many times since to enhance worship services, Bible schools, special programs, weddings, and even funerals at First Baptist and in other churches. Whenever they are used, they bring joy and assurance of the power in the name of the Lord to those in the audience. An invitation to join the banner ministry influenced one participant to become a member of First Baptist. She recalls hearing a member of a sister church who attended a banner program saying "That was the most worshipful experience I've ever had."[1] *Photo by Jonathan Canfield.*

---

1. Carolyn Driver, Interview with Nancy Dunn, April 8, 2008.

Members of the FBC youth choir, Ekklesia, present the gospel in song and through stick dramatizations.

Above: Ekklesia Stick Ministry—New Orleans tour, 2004. *Photo courtesy Andre Simon.*

increased significantly, as had giving to the SBC Cooperative Program, total annual giving, and gifts to missions.

Although not listed in his original fourteen objectives, Reed quickly observed that the church's central facilities were in need of major renovation and repair, and he wanted to get these underway prior to the congregation's centennial celebration of the church's founding. The architectural firm of Wiener, Hill, Morgan, O'Neal and Sutton was employed in February 1983, to develop a master plan for renovation. The architect identified ten needs, including exterior and interior repairs and renovation, remodeling the sanctuary, energy conservation, landscaping, a covered entry, and additional parking. The congregation approved the Master Renovation Plan in July. Because of the debt still owed on the Christian Life Center, Reed recommended the church not borrow any additional money and complete each project on a "pay-as-we-go" basis. By early fall the congregation was engaged in Partners in Progress, a campaign to raise funds to address the first items in the plan—exterior and interior renovation, repairs, and energy conservation. In time, the church addressed each of the needs listed by the architects. "Pay-as-we-go" continued to be the policy of the church for building projects and property acquisition until the Children's Building was constructed in 2003.

In 1984, First Baptist Church celebrated its one-hundredth birthday. A committee chaired by Rose Ann Pool contacted former pastors and staff members, compiled scrapbooks of church history, produced a stained glass window brochure, and commissioned a special insert for the *Daily Sentinel*. The year-long celebration began on Saturday evening, January 21, with a banquet in the Stephen F. Austin State University Center's Grand

Right: Ekklesia Choir—New Orleans tour, 2004. *Photo courtesy Andre Simon.*

Led by Loraine Young, the Lighthouse Singers present musical programs to residents of nursing homes and assisted living facilities in Nacogdoches. *Photo by Jimmy Partin.*

Ballroom. The banquet program featured a multimedia presentation of the church's history prepared by Mildred Sitton, George Thompson, and Bob Dunn. In addressing the congregation at the banquet, Dr. Reed commented that all the church had been, what it was then, and what it would become was all in God's hands, and he admonished the members present to "Never hesitate to trust an unknown future to a known God."[7] On Sunday morning a special worship service featured an anthem written specifically for the occasion by composer Eugene Butler. The celebration continued throughout the year as each living former pastor returned to fill the pulpit.

First Baptist Church's Christmas gift to the Nacogdoches community is a pageant of the Christmas storytelling of the ultimate Christmas gift, the birth of Jesus Christ. Under the leadership of Minister of Music Andre Simon, the Celebration Choir, the Celebration Orchestra, and the Drama Ministry Team work long hours throughout the fall months to prepare the presentation. *Photo by Jimmy Partin.*

Like his predecessors, Reed has been active in denominational and associational affairs. He served as a trustee of East Texas Baptist University in Marshall, Texas, and took an active role in the Shelby-'Doches Baptist Association, chairing the Stewardship and Evangelism committees, serving on the Baptist Student Union Committee, and chairing the spring simultaneous associational revivals in 1986, Good News America.

In the spring of 1988, Bobby Smith, First Baptist's minister for youth and university students, expanded the church's ministry to university students by beginning the Great Escape program on Wednesday evenings.

Latvian Mission—
"Baptist to Baptist"

In September 1991, after his native Latvia was freed from communist domination, Carlos Gruber led a team of First Baptist members to Latvia to conduct an evangelistic crusade. While there, team members learned about the poverty of Latvian Baptists, their great need for assistance in reestablishing their churches, and their need for even the basic necessities of life. After the team returned to Nacogdoches, Gruber's close friend and member of the team, L. D. Pate, enlisted the congregation of First Baptist Church in collecting supplies—clothing and nonperishable food items—to send to needy Baptists in Gruber's homeland. An eight-by-eight-by-forty-foot shipping container was located on the church's front lawn and quickly filled. That container was the first of a total of nine shipping containers filled with food, clothing, medicines, and medical equipment and sent to Latvia by First Baptist Church members and other Baptist congregations in the Shelby-'Doches and Rusk-Panola Baptist associations. Shipments sent at Christmas

L. D. Pate, the man who had the vision of helping Latvian Baptists by sending shipping containers to Latvia filled with food, clothing, and medicine. *Photo courtesy of Anita Standridge.*

time included toys and candies for the children in Latvian Baptist churches. This assistance to Latvian Baptists included financial support from the church budget, money contributed by First Baptist Church members and Sunday school classes, and contributions from Gruber Evangelistic Missions (GEM) supporters nationwide to renovate churches, provide meeting facilities for Latvian Baptists, and pay travel for the native pastors to minister to their congregations.

In 1993, First Baptist Church sent a team headed by Dr. Allen Reed to participate in the Latvian Church-to-Church Crusade. Additional teams from First Baptist Church followed later to do mission work with the Latvian

Above: One of the shipping containers sent to Latvia by First Baptist Church assisted by other congregations in the Shelby-'Doches Baptist Association. L. D. Pate, who chaired the project, is shown on the far right of the second row along with others who helped load the container. *Photo courtesy of Anita Standridge.*

Right: Matthew Baptist Church in Riga, Latvia, undergoing renovation with funds provided by First Baptist Church and other supporters of Gruber Evangelistic Ministries. *First Baptist Church Archives.*

pastors. As a result of participating on one of these teams, Dr. Bruce Cox, a local veterinarian and deacon of First Baptist Church, felt led to sell his veterinary practice and begin seminary studies to prepare for the ministry. These photographs show the group that loaded one of the containers, L. D. Pate—the guiding force in promoting First Baptist Church's involvement in Latvian missions, and one of the Latvian Baptist churches renovated with help from First Baptist Church. In fulfillment of the third part of its statement of purpose—*Finding the lost, Building the believer, Changing the world*—the church continued to provide support for the work of Latvian Baptists throughout Gruber's lifetime.

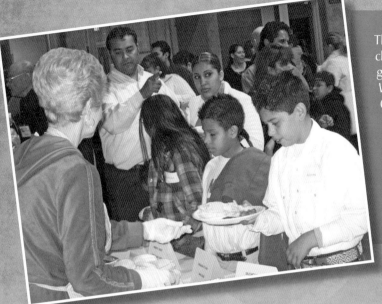

The Saturday performance of the Gift of Christmas, the church's Christmas pageant, is for the congregation's guests from the Christian Women's Job Corps, the Women's Shelter of East Texas, Heartbeat Pregnancy Center, Community RX Help, Nacogdoches Hope Food, Love, Inc., HOPE (Helping Others Practice English), and the American Red Cross. Guests are served a meal in the Christian Life Center prior to the program. After the pageant, each family receives a bag of groceries and an age-appropriate gift for each child in the family twelve years old and younger. Sue Sanders serves one of the families in December 2008. *Photo by Jimmy Partin.*

Every Sunday, deacon and Sunday school secretary Joe Biggerstaff makes pot after pot of "the best coffee at the best price in town" for members and guests of First Baptist Church. Along with each cup of coffee that he dispenses, Biggerstaff provides a quip or word of encouragement with a twinkle in his eye. Margaret Russell is shown being served by Biggerstaff. *Photo by Jimmy Partin.*

Originally organized as the GEM Class (G—gospel taught, E—everlasting life, M—maturing in the faith) in April 1988, the class was renamed the Fireside Class in January 1994 when it began meeting in the Fireside Room of the Christian Life Center. The class's original teacher was Jim McDonald, First Baptist Church's minister of administration/education. Its charter members were McDonald, Patricia Allen, and Carolyn and Bill Sylvester. By 2008, the class had a membership of ninety-four and a weekly attendance of approximately fifty. Dr. Mark Simmons became the teacher in 1994 when McDonald resigned as teacher to devote more time to the total Sunday school program. The Fireside Class was one of the first classes for couples at First Baptist. It focuses on teaching the Bible, singing familiar hymns, ministering to its members, and fellowship. *Photo by Jimmy Partin.*

Smith used his successful experience with Wednesday night Bible studies for middle school and high school students to tailor a praise and worship service specifically for the needs of university students. To avoid conflict with the other Wednesday evening activities at the church and at the Stephen F. Austin State University Baptist Student Ministry, Smith scheduled the service at 9:00 p.m., a time that proved ideal for university students. Beginning with about fifteen students gathered for pizza and informal Bible study, followed by shooting hoops in the gym, Great Escape quickly outgrew the capacity of the Christian Life Center game room and then the CLC basement, eventually moving into the church sanctuary and becoming a contemporary worship service that regularly attracts 400–500 students. Students sing, play instruments, and serve as worship leaders. Several of the student worship leaders have subsequently entered various phases of the ministry after their college days. One of these, David Reed, now First Baptist's youth minister, summarized the impact of the Great Escape ministry: "Many people . . . who have had opportunities to be a part in leadership at Great Escape . . . are out doing ministry now, and I think that Great Escape had a huge impact on them. . . . It's neat that I got to see it start and see where it all came from with just a [few] people sitting around some pizza having a Bible study to where it is now, a full blown worship experience."[8]

Reed felt led to begin additional ministries and expand the church staff to oversee them, but money to fund new programs was limited because of the large payments on the construction loan for the Christian Life Center and Preschool buildings. Reed was convinced that the best way for the church to move forward, establish additional programs, and hire staff to implement them was to become debt free, so he recommended paying off the remaining construction debt of $1,013,399. In October 1988, the Forward to Freedom Debt Reduction Campaign began with a banquet

Above left: First Baptist Church's commitment to ministering to the spiritual needs of the whole family includes providing quality teaching for even the youngest members of the congregation. Veteran Sunday school teachers Loraine Young, Donna Klemcke, and Leon Young teach preschool children about God's love. *Photo by Jimmy Partin.*

Above right: Jay and Amy Tullos teach first graders in the Children's Building, completed in 2005. *Photo by Jimmy Partin.*

"When I was in first grade, Mr. L. D. Pate was my Sunday school teacher. He called me on the telephone, just as he did each one in his class, every Saturday night to remind me that he was looking forward to seeing me the next morning in Sunday school."

Patricia (Redfield) Jones

Paul Cook Sunday School Class.
Photo by Jimmy Partin.

Russ Hairston Sunday School Class.
Photo by Jimmy Partin.

Ed Pool Sunday School Class.
Photo by Jimmy Partin.

Many husbands and wives attend Sunday school together as couples at First Baptist. Ed Pool teaches a class for couples with children, Paul Cook teaches a class for empty nesters and couples with older children, and Russ Hairston teaches a couples class for senior adults.

The Berean Ladies Class meets in the Hobby Room. Betty Sue Pruitt, Jean Rudisill, and Maggie Driggers share teaching responsibilities. *Photo by Jimmy Partin.*

Some women and men still prefer to have separate classes for Sunday school.

The Kerr Men's Class meets in the Ceramics Room and is taught by Jerry Sitton. *Photo by Jimmy Partin.*

Ministering to single, career adults is an important part of the mission of First Baptist Church. Teachers of the single adult Sunday school class are Jennifer and Mark Leuschner and Janice Haile. *Photo by Jimmy Partin.*

Teenagers love to eat. Juice and doughnuts are a regular Sunday morning Bible study feature for the middle school and high school departments, and the beginning of a new school year and a new Sunday school year calls for something special.

Above: Students served (right to left) are Sarah and Michelle Prince. *Photo by Jimmy Partin.*

in the Christian Life Center. By Thanksgiving, $302,746.42 had been raised, and less than four years later, on September 20, 1992, the congregation celebrated being debt free by burning the paid note in the morning worship service.

With the church's debt eliminated, Reed asked the congregation to redirect the money that had been required to pay the construction note to expanding the church's ministries and staff. A sixteen-member Long Range Planning Committee was appointed to review the needs of the church and make recommendations to the congregation. The committee's report, A New Vision, was adopted early in 1993. In addition to a formal statement of purpose, the report identified twenty-nine needs, three of which were recommended for immediate action—improve facilities for the handicapped and senior adults, increase emphasis on missions and personal involvement in missions, and strengthen the family in the church and the community.

Increased involvement in missions, especially international missions, was an almost immediate result of the committee's work. Under the leadership of the Reverend Carlos Gruber and L. D. Pate, the church began direct assistance to struggling Baptist congregations in Gruber's native Latvia, recently freed from Communist domination. Shipping containers of food, clothing, and medical supplies were sent to help meet the needs of the Latvian congregations. Money was donated to purchase and renovate

Right: Bryan Farrell (left) and David Russell (right) prepare pancakes for the youth Sunday school. *Photo by Jimmy Partin.*

From the beginning of Stephen F. Austin State University in 1923, members of First Baptist Church have conducted a student ministry. The church was instrumental in helping to secure a Baptist Bible Chair at the university and facilities to house the Baptist Student Union, now known as the Baptist Student Ministry. Ed Pool, First Baptist Church deacon shown at the BSM entrance, chaired the associational committee that purchased and remodeled a strip mall center adjacent to the campus for the new facility. *Photo by Jonathan Canfield.*

Ministering to the students of Stephen F. Austin State University is a priority of First Baptist Church. The University Sunday School Class meets in The Blend, an informal coffee house setting on the bottom floor of the Christian Life Center.

Associate Pastor and Minister to University Students Bobby Smith led a back-to-school Sunday morning Bible study for university students in September 2008. *Photo by Jimmy Partin.*

Jana Fehrle (far right), First Baptist Stephen F. Austin State University intern, welcomes fellow university students to the fall semester kick-off breakfast in 2008. *Photo by Jimmy Partin.*

"Mr. Joe"

Joe Jones, affectionately known as "Mr. Joe," was the "keeper of the keys" of First Baptist Church for thirty-five years. He began work as the church's building engineer in 1955 and retired in 1990 at the age of ninety-two. Prior to coming to work at First Baptist, Mr. Joe was a mechanic at an automobile dealership. When approached by three men from the congregation about coming to work for the church, Joe's response was "[Imagine that,] a grease monkey in the Baptist church!" He and his wife, Jimmie (Cleavenger), joined First Baptist in 1921, and, except for a brief period when they served as house parents at a boys' home in Round Rock, Texas, First Baptist Church was their church home.

Mrs. Jones taught nine-year-olds in Girls in Action for many years. Several members of the church today remember her and Mr. Joe driving them to G.A. camp in the summers. Before she died, Jimmie asked the deacons to "Take care of my Joe," and they did, providing him with work and an income long past the time when most employers would have encouraged him to retire. But Mr. Joe was no ordinary employee. He was more like a member of the family to the congregation as he greeted them warmly when they entered the building, helped carry their covered dishes and flower arrangements in and out of the building, and distributed orange slice candies to the day school children.

Growing up on an East Texas farm, Mr. Joe became accustomed to hard work at an early age. The oldest of eleven children, he never had time to attend school. As he explained, "As soon as I got big enough to keep the others pulled out of the fire, my daddy started me plowing and pulling up . . . sprouts. I just learned how to work." And work he did, arriving by 6:00 each morning to have the building unlocked, heated or cooled as the weather dictated, the lights on, and the coffee made by the time the rest of the staff arrived. Regardless of what day of the week, how long the day, or how late the committee meeting or choir rehearsal, Mr. Joe was always the last to leave, making sure the lights were out and the doors locked before he went home. In between performing his chores, he frequently could be seen with his pocket transistor radio keeping up with the news or listening to his favorite commentator, Paul Harvey.

With no children and no family members living nearby, the congregation became Mr. Joe's family and the church his home, especially after his wife's death in 1971. He loved the congregation and was dearly loved by them in return. During his tenure at the church, he served under eight of the church's twenty-two pastors. When Dr. Allen Reed came as the church's pastor, Mr. Joe took him to the north hallway where portraits of all the pastors who had served the congregation were hung. "Lookee there, preacher," he observed. "Don't none of 'em stay too long!" Dr. Reed proved to be the exception to Mr. Joe's observation; he was Mr. Joe's pastor for more than fifteen years. Mr. Joe died in October 1996, shortly after his ninety-eighth birthday. *First Baptist Church Archives.*

In fulfillment of the Biblical command to care for widows in the church, Bennat and Pat Mullen organized the Bridge Ministry in February 2006 to create a "bridge" over which members of the congregation could provide support and assistance to widowed members. Spring and fall car care days are among the many forms of help provided. Members of the ministry team check automobiles to be sure they are in proper operating condition. Left to right, Bennat Mullen, Pat Mullen, Larry Parkerson, Vi Hopper, Doyle Pittmon, Manuel Williams, Doyle Alexander, Elizabeth Biggers, Marilyn Barton, and Tom Hebert. *Photo by Jimmy Partin.*

church buildings, and teams of First Baptist members went to assist Latvian pastors in evangelistic meetings. In addition to Latvia, First Baptist has sent mission teams to Brazil, Mexico, France, Tanzania, Jamaica, and the Czech Republic during Reed's tenure as pastor.

Continuing its interest in establishing new Southern Baptist work, the church has sponsored three new Baptist churches under Reed's leadership. The Star of Hope Baptist Church was sponsored in 1984, Eden Baptist Church was sponsored in 1996, and Highway 259 (now Trinity)

Baptist Church was sponsored in 1998. In 1994, First Baptist provided financial support and sponsored the reorganization of Memorial Baptist Church, one of its original mission churches, into Iglesia Bautista Memorial to serve the growing Hispanic population in Nacogdoches. Fledgling Baptist churches in Kemmerer, Wyoming, and Pullman, Washington, have also received support from the membership of First Baptist.

In 1996, as the congregation looked forward to the twenty-first century, Reed asked the church to appoint a new Long Range Planning Committee to conduct a comprehensive study of the church's mission, strengths, and weaknesses. Adopted early in 1998, the committee's report, Vision 2000, reviewed and evaluated the church's achievement of its previous goals, reaffirmed the statement of purpose originally adopted in 1993, and recommended "*Finding the Lost, Building the Believer, Changing the World*" as a slogan to promote the church's overall mission. Seeds planted by this committee

In 1996, Brad Haile asked Bettye Alexander and Marilyn Barton to direct the Senior Adult Department for a few weeks until he could find someone to do the job on a permanent basis. In 2009 Bettye (third from left) and Marilyn (fourth from left) were still directing the Senior Adult Sunday School Department and ministering to senior adult members of First Baptist Church who reside in nursing homes and assisted living facilities. Arbor residents shown left to right are Ettie Cammack, Martha Dudley, and Ruth Martin. *Photo by Jimmy Partin.*

Each Sunday members of the congregation provide a floral arrangement for the Sunday morning worship services in memory or honor of loved ones or to commemorate special events. Early on Monday mornings, the members of the Flower Ministry divide the large arrangements into smaller bouquets and deliver them to church members who are residents of nursing homes or confined to their own homes. Committee members, left to right, are Barbara Jones, Larry Parkerson, Elizabeth Biggers, Vi Hopper, and Auderle Parkerson. *Photo by Jimmy Partin.*

eventually led to a recommendation by the Church Growth Committee to develop a long-range plan for church facilities and focus on constructing a building designed specifically to minister to young children and their families.

As the twentieth century drew to a close, all evangelical denominations experienced changes in forms of worship and ministry. Always less formal in worship than some other Protestant denominations, Baptists became even less formal. Musical genres and instruments not traditionally found in churches came into common use. New sound and visual technologies and religious drama were incorporated into worship services in an attempt to reach generations that grew to adulthood accustomed to television, computers, and cell phones. Worship services incorporating these forms were referred to as "contemporary." Not all First Baptist members embraced the new worship forms with enthusiasm. In an effort to maintain more traditional forms of worship while still meeting the needs and desires of younger members, the congregation added a second "blended" worship service prior to the Sunday school hour in 1993. By 1997, the congregation had returned to a single, more contemporary, morning worship service following Sunday school. In January 2007, the church resurrected the two-service format with an early blended traditional-contemporary service, *Celebration*. The second service, *The Gathering*, utilized the new, less formal music formats and instrumentation.

Late in 2005, the 9:00–10:00 a.m. Sunday morning broadcast time over television Channel 10, KTRE-TV, was made available to First Baptist after it was released by another East Texas Baptist congregation. The church had

Following in the footsteps of Dick Turner of First Baptist Church and Wilsey Clark of Fredonia Hill Baptist Church, Tip Harris began collecting outdated church literature and magazines and distributing them to inmates in the Nacogdoches County Jail in 1990. Since that time the jail ministry has grown to include holding regular devotional services in the jail as well as counseling and witnessing to individual inmates. Over the years Harris has led many inmates to a belief in Jesus Christ as their savior or to renew their faith. He is confident that, even when there are no visible results of his work, seeds have been sown that the Lord can use to change the lives of the inmates to whom he witnessed. In this photograph Harris witnesses to an inmate. *Photo courtesy of Tip Harris.*

Sometimes ministry can be as simple as providing a cool drink of water to hot, thirsty people. At the annual Nacogdoches Blueberry Festival, First Baptist Church members distribute ice-cold bottles of water along with information about Jesus Christ, the living water. Shown giving water to a festival attendee is Travis Clark. *Photo by Jonathan Canfield.*

Each year the deacon body honors the widows of First Baptist Church deacons with a fellowship meal. Shown left to right are deacon Durwood Henry, Mary Henry, deacon Johnny Rusidill, and deacon widows Ann Sweat, Vi Hopper, and Eloise Greenville. *Photo by Jimmy Partin.*

In 1991, the members of First Baptist Church began an intercessory prayer ministry in honor of Dr. Allen Reed's tenth anniversary as the church's pastor and in fulfillment of his vision that First Baptist would be a praying church. A room just inside the south entrance to the church was renovated and dedicated to this purpose. In the room are kept lists of prayer needs of the church family, the community, and people around the world. These needs are often communicated by church members, but are not restricted to members of the congregation. The Prayer Room is available twenty-four hours a day, every day of the week for the fifty or more volunteer "prayer warriors" who come and spend an hour praying for these needs and for the church. Seated at the desk in the prayer room is Prayer Room Ministry coordinator Jean Rudisill. *Photo by Tom Atchison.*

The Women's Ministry

The first formal women's organization of First Baptist Church was the Women's Missionary Society, organized during the ministry of the congregation's fifth pastor, Thomas Bunyan Harrell. Harrell's wife, Josephine, was the first WMS president. The ladies of the WMS promoted missions and conducted Bible studies in Nacogdoches neighborhoods and communities in the county. Two of these Bible studies, one in the Fredonia Hill neighborhood and one in the Spanish-speaking Bonaldo community, led to the establishment of mission churches by First Baptist. Over time the name of the WMS was changed to the Women's Missionary Union, or WMU. It continued to be a strong organization throughout the twentieth century as WMU "circles" of ladies met during the day and in the evenings to accommodate the busy schedules of the women of the church. The circles studied about and supported all forms of missions—local, state, North American, and international. They promoted the Week of Prayer for Missions and the annual

These ladies were leaders in the First Baptist Women's Missionary Union during the mid-twentieth century. Shown seated, left to right on the first row, are Sallie T. Summers and Lorene Dorsey. On the second row, left to right, are Grace Monk, Kathleen Campbell, Noel Thompson, Ruby Tannery, and Agnes Rogers (seated). Other WMU leaders not pictured include Lois Stripling, Edna Earl Reese, Christine Jones, Annette Crawford, Edna Jackson, Frances Rudisill, Dimple Gound, Ruth Cooksey, and Mary Bass Rhodes. *First Baptist Church Archives.*

offerings for state, home, and international missions, and sponsored the work of mission organizations for children and youth—Mission Friends, Girls Auxiliary, Acteens, and Royal Ambassadors. In addition, the ladies of the WMU frequently planned and prepared receptions for the arrival and departure of church staff members. Mary (Bass) Rhodes characterized the WMU of that era as being "the strong arm of the church."[1]

An annual ladies retreat, or "Spring Fling," was begun in 1981 to provide a time of spiritual renewal for the women of the church and an outreach to the community. Well-known Christian speakers such as Beth Moore, Beverly LaHaye, and Marge Caldwell have been featured at the retreats.

In March 2000, the First Baptist Women's Missions and Ministry was organized to serve as an umbrella organization for all of the women's groups of the church. Stacia Prince was its first president. The WMM seeks to provide opportunities for spiritual growth for women and to equip them to minister to their families, the church body, the community, and the world through retreats, Bible studies, fellowships, mentorships, mission activities, and conferences. The WMM sponsors the HOPE Angel program to provide Christmas gifts to the children of students in Helping Others Practice English classes, Bible studies and Easter egg hunts for the children of the Commonwealth Apartment Complex, and provides meals for the Baptist Student Ministry at Stephen F. Austin State University. Along with women from other churches in Nacogdoches, the WMM helps provide teachers, mentors, lunches, childcare, and clothing for participants in the Christian Women's Job Corps, a ministry begun by First Baptist member Melba Tiller.

1. Mary Bass Rhodes, Interview with Jean Rudisill, March 4, 2008.

"THE WOMEN'S MISSIONARY UNION IS THE STRONG ARM OF THE CHURCH."
Mary Bass Rhodes

In 2002, the First Baptist Women's Missions and Ministry sponsored a holiday retreat, "Redeeming the Season," led by authors Kim Wier and Pam McCune. The retreat's purpose was to help the women of the church and community make Jesus Christ the focus of their Christmas celebrations and to lead them to build meaningful holiday traditions around his birth. Hostesses of the retreat were, left to right, Caroline Garner, Raquel Skidmore, Jane Ferren, Stacy Adkins, Leslie Heard, Krecia Pierce, Catherine Russell, Simonetta Gowan, Donna Jones, Angela Howarth, Pat Warner, and Christie Barber. *Photo courtesy of Simonetta Gowan.*

The Younger Olders, an active group of First Baptist Church senior adults, meets regularly for meals, fellowship, and dominos. *Photo courtesy of Younger Olders.*

In a tradition begun by Dr. Archie McDonald in 1967, members of First Baptist Church gather annually on the Sunday evening closest to July 4 to celebrate our nation's independence and freedom of worship with a picnic that includes hot dogs, hamburgers, and, of course, sliced watermelon. *Photo by Jonathan Canfield.*

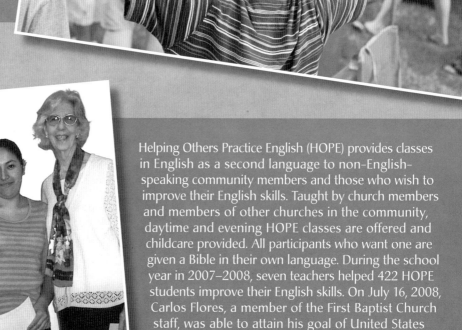

Helping Others Practice English (HOPE) provides classes in English as a second language to non-English-speaking community members and those who wish to improve their English skills. Taught by church members and members of other churches in the community, daytime and evening HOPE classes are offered and childcare provided. All participants who want one are given a Bible in their own language. During the school year in 2007–2008, seven teachers helped 422 HOPE students improve their English skills. On July 16, 2008, Carlos Flores, a member of the First Baptist Church staff, was able to attain his goal of United States citizenship as a result of his enrollment in HOPE. Baylor University and the *Baptist Standard* recently presented the Marie Mathis Award for Lay Ministry to Robin Fieistal, the first director of the HOPE ministry. Left to right, are Kerry Lemon (teacher), Julia Garcia, Socorro Garcia, and Maggie Driggers (teacher). *Photo courtesy of Maggie Driggers.*

televised the morning worship service over the ACTS subscription cable television network briefly in 1991, but cost and the limited audience caused the broadcast to be discontinued after only a few months. This time, however, the service could be broadcast to the entire area served by the station. Since the available time slot did not coincide with the Sunday morning worship service schedule, it was necessary to record the service for broadcast the

The Whitehead sisters, Hazel (Hay), left, and Gladys (Mimi), right, were honored by First Baptist and their pastor, Allen Reed (rear), as the Mothers of the Year on Mother's Day, 1983. Although they never married and had children of their own, they raised eight children during their lifetimes. After their mother's death in 1928, they cared for their five younger brothers and sisters. Later, when their sister died in 1947, they took her three children, Darla (Whitton) Shirley, David Whitton, and Linda (Whitton) Fisher, into their home. The two sisters worked in the preschool Sunday school department for many years where they shared God's love with the children of the congregation. *Nacogdoches Daily Sentinel.*

following Sunday. Funds were donated to equip a recording studio in the church basement and install cameras in the sanctuary, and volunteers were trained to record and edit the services for rebroadcast.

As the church began to embrace the digital age and utilize more technology in ministry, the need for a full-time media specialist to oversee the total communication program of the church became apparent. In 2007, Jonathan Canfield, who grew up attending First Baptist, became the

Elton Alexander was recognized by the congregation as the Father of the Year on June 21, 1992. Alexander and his wife, Lillian, joined First Baptist Church in 1934, and he was ordained a deacon in 1947. He taught the nine-year-old boys' Sunday school class for thirty-one years—two generations in some church families—and worked with the Royal Ambassador organization. During his recognition many men in the congregation stood to acknowledge the influence he had on their lives as their teacher or RA leader. Alexander and his wife were the parents of one son, Earl, and two daughters, Beth Howell and Faye Matlock. Left to right, Lillian Alexander, Dr. Allen Reed, Elton Alexander, and Dr. and Mrs. Earl Alexander. *First Baptist Church Archives.*

As a result of close association with Terry and Twylia Bell, Southern Baptist Convention missionaries to Tanzania, church members became aware of the need of missionary families on stateside assignment to have a comfortable, furnished home. Under the leadership of Associate Pastor Bobby Smith, the congregation purchased a lot in the Colonial Hills subdivision and constructed and fully furnished a house where missionary families can live during their time on furlough. In 2003, the Terry Bell family became the first missionaries to live in the home. First Baptist Church member and contractor Kerry Powell supervised the construction of the house.

The Missionary House. *Photo by Jonathan Canfield.*

Kerry Powell working on the missionary house. *First Baptist Church Archives.*

In the summers of 2007 and 2008, church members witnessed to and helped construct homes for poverty-stricken people in the Caribbean nation of Jamaica. First Baptist Church Minister of Administration and Senior Adults Brad Haile presents a Jamaican man with a Bible and the keys to his new home. *Photo courtesy of Bobby Smith.*

First Baptist Church provides opportunities for its middle and high school youth to experience missions. In the summer of 2008, thirteen First Baptist Church youth and leaders, led by youth minister David Reed, participated in a World Changers mission trip to minister to the Roma people of Ostrava, Czech Republic, in central Europe. Bret Partin, one of the team members, poses with Roma boys that participated in the organized sports and Bible study provided by the team. *Photo courtesy of David Reed.*

First Baptist Church regularly sends mission teams to assist resident Southern Baptist missionaries in many parts of the world. Recent First Baptist efforts have focused on helping the International Mission Board missionary Terry Bell and the Shinyanga, Tanzania, Baptist Association.

"OTHERS IN THE CHURCH HAVE GONE [ON MISSION TRIPS] AND HELPED WITH CHURCH PLANTING, PRACTICING EVANGELISM, PRAYER WALKING, ETC. I WENT IN MY PROFESSION AS AN AGRONOMIST, AND THIS IS WHERE GOD WANTED ME. IT'S SPECIAL TO KNOW THAT GOD IS USING US TO HELP SUKUMA FARMERS GROW A LITTLE MORE CORN AND HOPEFULLY LIVE A LITTLE BETTER."

Dr. Leon Young

The Africa Mission Team conducted house-to-house witnessing with the Shinyanga Baptist Association pastors in villages surrounding Shinyanga in 2007. Shown from left to right on the front row are team members Charlotte Wooton, Elizabeth Rodrigues, Molly Young, Jackie Pierce, Gary Russell, and Jimmy Partin. Pastors of the Shinyanga Baptist Association are shown on the second row. *Photo by Jimmy Partin.*

Charlotte Wooton on the way to an African village in the Shinyanga Province of northern Tanzania. *Photo by Jimmy Partin.*

In 2005, hurricanes Rita and Katrina, and again in 2008, hurricanes Gustav and Ike sent many evacuees to East Texas. First Baptist Church joined other congregations in Nacogdoches to shelter evacuees. *Photo by Jimmy Partin.*

Evacuees from hurricane Gustav eat in the Christian Life Center Hobby Shop. *Photo by Jimmy Partin.*

First Baptist members (left to right) Lena Funai, Betty Gayler, and Sue Sanders serve a meal to hurricane Gustav evacuees. *Photo by Jimmy Partin.*

church's first director of media and communications, responsible for editing the worship services for broadcast, creating PowerPoint presentations for services, managing the church web site, www.fbcnac.org, providing DVDs and CDs of services, formatting church bulletins, and producing the monthly newsletter, *First Family Focus.*

The format of Sunday evening services also changed. Many Baptist congregations discontinued them altogether. In an effort to meet the needs of the church family and utilize the talents of its members, First Baptist began offering a menu of small group workshop options on Sunday evenings. Named POPS—Preparing Our People for Service—the workshops, taught by the congregation, were correlated with the school calendar. Different topics were offered in fall and spring, and the meetings were discontinued during summer vacation. The pastor continued to offer a more traditional Sunday evening worship service focused on Bible teaching as an alternative to the POPS sessions. By 2006, the Sunday evening small group sessions had evolved into a less formal format with groups meeting in members' homes and focusing on enlisting friends and neighbors in Bible study. There was still a demand for the pastor's Sunday evening Bible study, so the Sunday evening service continued.

In the latter decades of the twentieth century, the Southern Baptist Convention and the Baptist General Convention of Texas were torn by doctrinal disagreements between factions labeled Moderates and Fundamentalists. The struggle between these groups for control of the conventions divided many Baptist congregations. Reed refused to get involved in the political struggles for control of the machinery of the con-

The Terry Bell Family

First Baptist Church's own international missionaries are Terry and Twylia Bell. Terry was baptized, met his wife, ordained a deacon, and surrendered to international missions, all at First Baptist Church. After working in the Soils Laboratory at Stephen F. Austin State University for fourteen years, Terry felt called to enter the mission field. Assigned by the Southern Baptist Convention's International Mission Board to Shinyanga, Tanzania, to work in agricultural and church development, Terry established an agricultural training center to introduce modern farming methods to the local

Sukuma people, many of whom are subsistence farmers, and to provide leadership development for the local Baptist pastors.

Throughout their tenure on the mission field, First Baptist Church has remained the Bells' home church, and the congregation has provided them prayer and financial support. During their time in Shinyanga, the church has sent five mission teams to minister to and work with the Bells. The teams have done prayer-walking and door-to-door witnessing in the villages, preached in the village churches, conducted Bible schools for national and missionary family children, and worked with Tanzanian university ministries. In addition, the church and the Kerr Men's Sunday School Class have provided funds for the improvement of church facilities, usually mud-brick structures, in the Shinyanga Baptist Association. "Each time the teams have come, they have been used greatly by the Lord" said Bell. "The people, pastors, and church leaders are encouraged a great deal."[1] The people of Tanzania and especially of the Shinyanga Baptist Association, he says, have a great love for First Baptist Church and want the church to continue to send mission teams to work with them.

Shown in front of First Baptist Church's mission house where they reside when on stateside assignment are Terry, Twylia, Amanda (a student at East Texas Baptist University in Marshall, Texas), Jaree (who was born in Africa), and Lance. In May 2008, the Bells returned to Tanzania to begin a new work with the Ngoni people group in the Songea area of southern Tanzania. *Photo by Jonathan Canfield.*

---

1. Terry Bell. Interview with Jean Rudisill, March 25, 2008.

First Baptist Church members who experience the birth of a child bring their new baby before the congregation and dedicate themselves to rearing their child in a Christian home and teaching them about God. At the same time, the congregation pledges to lift up the parents and their children in prayer. *First Baptist Church Archives.*

ventions because he believed these battles were a distraction from Baptists achieving their mission of reaching a lost world for Jesus Christ. Following their pastor's leadership, First Baptist Church avoided becoming entangled in doctrinal controversies. As a result, although First Baptist Church leans strongly toward being theologically fundamentalist, some other members of the local Baptist association consider the church to be theologically moderate because it never formally aligned with the fundamentalist faction. Not taking sides in this controversy, however, made it possible for First Baptist to maintain its focus on its stated purpose of *"Finding the Lost, Building the Believer, Changing the World."*

Watched by a host of moms, dads, and fellow church members, the children of First Baptist Church stand ready with their toy shovels on November 9, 2003, to break ground for the new Children's Building. *First Baptist Church Archives.*

On Friday, March 26, 1998, while at his desk working on his Sunday morning message, Reed began to experience pain in his shoulder. When it moved to his back and chest, he called his wife to take him to the doctor. His doctor told him he was having a heart attack and personally rushed him to the hospital where it was discovered that he had blockages in four coronary arteries. After he was stabilized, Reed was taken to St. Luke's Hospital in Houston, Texas, where he received three coronary bypasses. During his recovery the Reverend Bobby Smith assumed Reed's preaching responsibilities. On November 7, only a few months after he returned to work, one of Reed's bypasses blocked and he was again rushed to the hospital. Once again, Smith filled the pulpit during Reed's recovery. On both of these occasions, the congregation rallied behind their pastor and assumed more responsibility for ministering to fellow church members and to the community. When Reed recovered and returned to work, the church encouraged him to reduce his workload by delegating more of his responsibilities to other members of the church staff, and the membership

On November 9, 2003, a groundbreaking ceremony was held for the Children's Building. Turning shovelfuls of dirt are Children's Minister Tracy McGowan (center) and (left to right) Children's Building Committee members Jean Rudisill, Annelle Barbin, Lisa Mize, and Steve Crow. *First Baptist Church Archives.*

It was an exciting day in 2004 when the steel framework of the Children's Building began to take shape. *First Baptist Church Archives.*

In the modern world, parents want to know that their child will be safe when left in the care of others. When bringing their child to activities in the Children's Building, parents or others on the authorized list sign children in and out of the building on a computerized touch screen system at the Children's Building Welcome Desk. In this way the church member working at the desk always knows which children are in the building and who brought them. Parents of preschool children are issued a pager at check-in so that they may be easily summoned from other parts of the church plant if needed by their child. Robin Hancock checks her child into the building with Christel Long at the Welcome Desk. *Photo by Jimmy Partin.*

Men's Ministry

Men of First Baptist Church have consistently been involved in ministry throughout the church's history. Frequently their involvement has been a part of a formal organization, but just as often it has been as individual Christians and without publicity or fanfare.

In the fall of 1944, the Baptist Brotherhood movement began. By June 1945, First Baptist Church had an organized Brotherhood of thirty-two members with Pat Jackson as its president. Other original officers included George Hawkes, first vice-president, Ezra Prince, second vice-president, Emory Johnson, secretary, and Rufus Miller, treasurer. This organization remained strong for many years, with its members meeting for Bible study, fellowship, and to perform works of ministry for the church and the community. One of its greatest contributions in the local church was to promote missions and work with boys and young men in the Royal Ambassador organization.

Pat Jackson was the first president of the First Baptist Brotherhood organized in 1945. *First Baptist Church Archives.*

Although the Baptist Brotherhood began to wane as a denominational organization during the latter decades of the twentieth century, the men of the church continued to be involved in ministry. Like the Brotherhood, the First Baptist Church Men's Ministry meets for fellowship meals and Bible study, but they also go out into the community and the world to minister to the needs of others, often in conjunction with the women of the church. Some are active in other denominational organizations such as Texas Baptist Men, and others participate in ministries and projects of the local congregation. Many are involved in community-based service organizations and projects such as the American Red Cross, Helping Other People Eat, and Habitat for Humanity. Mission teams have helped Tanzanian subsistence farmers learn more efficient farming techniques, preached and witnessed in the mud-brick homes and churches in the Tanzanian countryside, and built greenhouses to help Jamaican nationals become more self-supporting.

First Baptist men have helped build homes for low income families, cleaned up and repaired churches on the storm-ravaged Texas coast, provided food, showers, and clean clothes in communities hit by natural disasters, fitted hearing aids on deaf children in Haiti, and done minor home repairs for widows and the elderly. They have visited the sick in hospitals and nursing homes, performed automobile checks for the widows of the congregation, distributed food to needy families, built a house for missionary families to use while on stateside assignment, fried turkeys so poor families could have a Christmas dinner, handed out water to thirsty tourists, and done hundreds of other things to show God's love for mankind.

Before his death from cancer, Jeff Kendrick organized men of First Baptist and their wives to cook turkeys and pans of dressing for delivery to needy families at Christmas. *Photo courtesy of Kalin Kendrick.*

Much of mission work is simply showing God's love for people by the actions of the mission team members. Here Gary Russell, a veteran of three Africa mission trips, carries the child of a member of one of the village churches in the Shinyanga Baptist Association. *Photo by Jimmy Partin.*

Children begin to learn of God's love through the love shown by adults in their lives. The First Baptist Church nursery staff, coordinated by Debbie Crenshaw, is committed to providing an environment in which each child's awareness of God's love for them is nurtured. Crenshaw holds Emma Hays (left) and Margie Lewallen (right). *Photo by Jimmy Partin.*

continued its involvement in ministry to further relieve their pastor's workload.

On Sunday, March 4, 2001, the congregation celebrated Reed's twentieth anniversary as the church's pastor and presented him and his wife with a tour of the Holy Land, a fulfillment of one of his lifelong dreams. Several members of the congregation joined the couple for the tour led by Dr. Bill Tolar, one of Reed's professors at Southwestern Baptist Seminary. After he returned Reed frequently used his experiences on this trip in his sermons.

Vision 2000, adopted by the congregation in 1998, recommended appointing a committee to evaluate the existing church facilities and make recommendations for future needs. A nine-member Church Growth Committee, chaired by Dr. Langston Kerr, was appointed in the spring of 2000. After a yearlong study, the committee identified a master plan as a major need and recommended the employment of Hatfield and Holcomb, Architects of Dallas, Texas, to develop one. Adopted by the congregation on September 15, 2002, the plan called for renovating existing facilities and beginning a four-phase building program to meet current and future needs. Phase one was the construction of a new building to meet the needs of the church's growing membership and to be an outreach to families with young children. Ministering to children had always been a high priority of First Baptist,

Children's Sunday school workers Erin and John Wyatt are shown with First Baptist Church children they "rounded up" for the beginning of a new Sunday school year. *Photo by Jonathan Canfield.*

One of the children's favorite activities in their new building is the slide. Children enter the slide through a large blue whale's mouth on the upper floor and exit on the ground floor. Emily Durham is shown flying out of the whale. *Photo by Jonathan Canfield.*

Two-year-olds enjoy snack time at Sunday school in the summer of 2008. *Photo by Jimmy Partin.*

In 2007, the five-year-old Vacation Bible School class had a sports theme. *First Baptist Church Archives.*

Mission Friends leaders (left to right) Amy Durham, Christel Long, Megan Tong, and Allison Inman teach young children familiar Bible stories and how missionaries tell other people about Jesus. *Photo by Jimmy Partin.*

Honoring their moms at the Royal Ambassadors Mother–Son Banquet are, left to right, Ben Augustine and mom Michelle; Clay Hayes and mom Lauree; Matthew Dillon and mom Marcia; Jake Morton and mom Diane. *Photo by Jonathan Canfield.*

After learning about missions, Royal Ambassadors learn archery and air rifle marksmanship and safety taught by leader Mike McClellan. Collin Long watches as McClellan demonstrates with an air rifle. *Photos by Jonathan Canfield.*

but employing a children's minister in 1997, and planning a new building specifically to meet the needs of children, was visible evidence of the congregation's commitment to children and their families.

Phase two of the master plan addressed improving access to existing church facilities, expanding parking, and acquiring additional property adjoining the church. Phases three and four called for construction of a new sanctuary and remodeling of the existing sanctuary to provide additional educational space when warranted by the growth of the congregation.

The Church Growth Committee, with the addition of four members, was asked to continue serving as a building committee for the construction of the children's building and the other projects in phase one. On November 10, 2002, H–H Architects were employed to design a building of approximately 22,000 square feet to house programs for children and their parents. J. E. Kingham Construction Company was designated construction manager at risk for the project. The Baptist General Convention of Texas *United We Build* program guided the fund-raising campaign that successfully solicited $3.5 million in gifts and pledges for the project from church members.

On Sunday, November 9, 2003, the children of the church participated in breaking ground for the construction of the first new facility built by First Baptist since the Christian Life Center twenty years earlier. By February 6, 2005, the building was finished and a dedication held. When parents and their children enter the building, they are greeted by a mural showing Jesus with modern-day children that illustrates the facility's mission—to teach children about God's love for them. Additional colorful wall murals showing familiar Bible stories are located throughout the building. Sunday school rooms for the parents of young children are located on the building's third floor, so they may attend their own Sunday school classes in the same building with their children. Having programs and a facility to meet the needs of families with young children has proven to be an effective ministry and community outreach for First Baptist.

In addition to constructing the Children's Building, the church sanctuary, chapel, lower auditorium, parlor, office, and middle and high school departments have all been renovated during Reed's tenure. North and south porte cocheres have been added to the main building, parking lots constructed to the north and south, and a circular drive extended

Leader Melanie Matson encourages Acteens (girls in grades 6–12) to become personally involved in mission projects. Each fall the girls enlist Mission Friends, Royal Ambassadors, Girls Auxiliary, and the entire church family in filling shoeboxes with gifts for distribution worldwide by Operation Christmas Child, a ministry of Franklin Graham's Samaritan's Purse organization. Included in each box is a copy of the Gospel of Luke in the recipient's own language. In 2008, the congregation filled 264 boxes, the most ever. *Photo courtesy of Melanie Matson.*

Summer youth camps such as Centrifuge are an integral part of the youth
ministry at First Baptist Church. Summer
camps serve First Baptist Church youth
and are an outreach to other youth in
the community. In the summer of 2008,
youth in grades 7–12 and their adult
leaders attended Centrifuge at Glorieta,
New Mexico. *Photo courtesy of David Reed.*

Acteens Jaclyn Partin (left) and
Karli Jones (right) help paint
a house as a service project
for Buckner Eldercare. *Photo
courtesy of Melanie Matson.*

The ordained deacons of First Baptist
Church are committed to being servants
in ministry and not a "board of directors."
First Baptist Church deacons are involved
in all of the church's ministries, as they
provide support and leadership for the
ministerial staff and the entire congregation. *Photo by Jonathan Canfield.*

The First Baptist ministerial staff and their spouses are, left to right, Brad Haile, minister of administration and senior adults, and Janice Haile; Andre Simon, minister of music, and Ronna Simon; Allen Reed, pastor, and Linda Reed; Bobby Smith, associate pastor and student minister, and Laura Smith; David Reed, minister of youth, and Kristie Reed; Melanie Matson, children's minister, and Craig Matson; and Jonathan Canfield, director of media and communications and fiancée Becca Mackey. *Photo by John Alvin Woods.*

"I AM TRULY THANKFUL TO BE A PART OF THIS GREAT CHURCH THAT HAS SUCH A LOVING, PRAYING GROUP OF MINISTERS AND STAFF AND MEMBERS WITH A GENUINE HEART FOR MISSIONS."

Anita (Pate) Standridge

The church office staff ensures that the daily functions of the church are carried out and the needs of the members met. From left to right, front row: Beverly Parrish, receptionist and church secretary, and Stephanie Van Dyke, Christian Life Center secretary. Second row: Barbara Breazeale, music and children's secretary; Rana Hillis, pastor's secretary; and Brenda Howard, administrative assistant. *Photo by Jonathan Canfield.*

One of the hallmarks of The Reverend Allen Reed's pastorate is the stability of the church staff. During his tenure as pastor of First Baptist Church, Reed has had only four secretaries. Two of these, seated Mary Cunningham (21 years) and standing Emily Holden (5½ years), served a total of nearly twenty-seven of Reed's twenty-eight years as pastor. *Photo by Jonathan Canfield.*

Cleaning and preparing the church plant for worship services and other weekly activities is a major task for a facility as large as First Baptist Church. Members of the church staff who perform this ministry faithfully and their years of service to 2009 are, left to right, Earl Gregory (19 years), Juana Landeros (4 years), and Carlos Flores (7 years). *Photo by Jonathan Canfield.*

from the north parking lot to improve access to the elevator for the elderly and handicapped.

As it became available, adjoining property has been purchased, and the church lot now extends from north of Baxter-Duncan Street almost to Hospital Street on the south and west to Pearl Street.

Longevity of staff has been a hallmark of Reed's pastorate and has contributed significantly to the stability of the church in recent years. The average tenure of the 2008–2009 ministerial staff is almost twelve years. One member of the ministerial staff, Bobby Smith, has tenure of twenty-six years, only two fewer than Reed. Another, staff member Brad Haile, has tenure of eighteen years. Two members of the support staff, Brenda Howard and Beverly Parrish, have tenures of twenty-eight and twenty-seven years, respectively, and during his twenty-eight years as pastor, Reed has had only four secretaries. One of these, Mary Cunningham, served as his secretary for twenty-one years.

In 2008, based on the premise that a church is not an *organization* but an *organism*—a living body of believers that is alive and growing—the membership of First Baptist continued to look to the future, even as they prepared to celebrate their 125-year past. A new seventeen-member Planning and Development Committee was appointed to identify and propose goals for the next five years. The committee and the ministerial staff conducted a needs assessment, surveyed the membership, consulted with the Baptist General Convention of Texas' strategist for church growth, and submitted its recommendations for the church to consider. On January 11, 2009, the congregation approved the committee's report, First Baptist Church Grows, and quickly began to address priority recommendations.

The library of First Baptist Church is a valuable source of Christian print and audiovisual media with selections for all age groups. Library volunteers Pat Smith (30 years service) and Donna Cook (14 years service) maintain the collection of 6,225 volumes and the computerized card catalog and circulation system. During the library's most recent summer reading program, they helped forty children read 580 books. The church's pastor, Dr. Allen Reed, is well known for his affinity for books. While a student in Southwestern Seminary, he worked in the seminary bookstore. Whenever new shipments of books arrived, Reed would examine them carefully and then place several on the "Allen Reed" shelf. On payday, he often endorsed his paycheck and returned it to the bookstore to pay for his purchases. In 2006, the congregation named the church library the Charles Allen Reed Library in recognition of Dr. Reed's love for books and in honor of his twenty-fifth anniversary as pastor. *Photo by Jimmy Partin.*

At 125 years old, First Baptist Church of Nacogdoches, Texas, is one of 1,193 congregations in the Baptist General Convention of Texas that have existed for one hundred years or more. During its history, the church has experienced significant growth in all areas. From the little group of thirteen believers organized into a church by Luther Rice Scruggs in the spring of 1885, the congregation has grown to almost 2,500 members, the largest in the forty-six-member Shelby-'Doches Baptist Association. From a pastor as the only staff member, the ministerial staff has grown to seven, with a support staff of nine. From the original white frame building and lot that cost $950 in 1886, the church plant has grown to a multi-building facility valued at $15 million in 2008. Giving to support the work of the local church and of Baptist denominational work has also grown during First Baptist's 125 years. The church's original budget was whatever the members contributed from Sunday to Sunday. In 2008, budget receipts totaled $1,999,593—only $500 less than $2 million. From the modest offering of $1.25 that Scruggs took to the associational meeting in 1886, the congregation's contribution to the Southern Baptist Convention's Cooperative Program has grown to just under $200,000 for 2008, and special mission offerings to more than $62,000 annually.

On Saturday, February 7, and Sunday, February 8, 2009, members, former members, and friends of First Baptist Church gathered to celebrate the 125th anniversary of the church's founding. Rose Ann Pool, who chaired the church's centennial celebration committee in 1984, was again called on to chair the planning committee. On Saturday evening more than five hundred people enjoyed a time of food, fellowship, and

"THE FIRST BAPTIST CHURCH FAMILY PROVIDES ME WITH SUPPORT, LOVE, AND CHRISTIAN FELLOWSHIP."

Marilyn Barton

Carlos Gruber, "Missionary to the World"

Charles Arthur (Carlos) Gruber, a native of Latvia, served as First Baptist's missionary to the world for almost half a century. As a young child in a poor Latvian family, Carlos received a jacket and cap from a shipment of clothing sent to Latvia by American Baptists. This gift made a lasting impression on Gruber, and he was forever grateful to the United States, a nation that later became his adopted country.

When Latvia was taken into the sphere of the Soviet Union following World War I, Gruber and his family, along with about two thousand other Latvians, immigrated to Brazil. He attended the Baptist College in Sao Paulo where he met Dr. Lee Scarborough, president of Southwestern Baptist Theological Seminary in Fort Worth, Texas. Dr. Scarborough invited Gruber to come to the United States and enroll in the seminary. After he was graduated from Southwestern, the beginning of World War II prevented Gruber from returning to Brazil, so he pastored a Latvian Baptist church in New York City, preached, and played his violin in evangelistic meetings. During this period Gruber also published a Latvian language newspaper exposing the hardships of the Latvian people under Communist rule, resulting in his being placed on a list of individuals marked for elimination by the Communist Party of the Soviet Union.

During a revival meeting in the First Baptist Church of Barstow, Florida, Gruber met Vivian Mercer, who became his wife and partner in ministry. In 1965, Vivian, a professor of modern languages, accepted a teaching position at Stephen F. Austin State University, and the Gruber family moved to Nacogdoches and joined First Baptist Church. With his ability to speak several languages, to preach, sing, and play the violin, Gruber was in constant demand as a missionary evangelist and frequently called upon by the Southern Baptist Convention's Foreign Mission Board to lead special crusades in many foreign countries.

In 1971, his Gruber Evangelistic Missions (GEM) received a charter from the State of Texas and became an official nonprofit organization to promote worldwide mission work. For the next thirty years, Gruber channeled contributions to GEM into evangelistic and Christian humanitarian efforts around the world. In 1991, after his homeland of Latvia was freed of Communist domination, Gruber concentrated his efforts on helping Latvian Baptists reestablish their churches and Christian work there.

In 1999, President Vaira Vika-Freiberga of Latvia recognized Gruber's efforts on behalf of his native land by designating him a Knight of the Three Stars, the Latvian nation's highest civilian honor. In this photograph, Gruber and his wife Vivian, along with Dr. Allen Reed, look at the award he received from his native country of Latvia.

In 2004, on Gruber's ninety-fourth birthday, his son, Charles Arthur Gruber Jr., paid the following tribute to his father: "I do not believe that there will ever be another person so dedicated to missions and evangelism."[1] Gruber died on July 8, 2004. His wife and partner in the GEM ministry died less than a year later, on May 8, 2005. *First Baptist Church Archives.*

---

1. Charles Arthur Gruber Jr., *Newsbreezes*. Nacogdoches, Texas, January/February 2004.

remembering the past at a banquet held in the Fredonia Hotel Convention Center. On Sunday morning a crowd of more than seven hundred gathered in the church sanctuary to enjoy special music, hear former pastors Dr. Bill Austin and Dr. Lionel Crowell recall memories of their time at First Baptist, and listen to the pastor, Dr. Allen Reed, preach on "Advancing the Kingdom." Reed reminded the congregation that Carlos Gruber often prayed for First Baptist Church to be a lighthouse in East Texas, and he exhorted them to continue being a faithful lighthouse for Jesus in the future, both in the community and wherever they should go. "Share what's in your heart." Reed said. "That's the essence of what being a Christian is—having Jesus in your heart and sharing him with others."

In reflecting on more than a quarter century as pastor of the same congregation, Allen Reed commented that as a young pastor he had dreamed of serving a long pastorate

On Saturday, February 7, 2009, members, former members, and friends of First Baptist Church gathered at the Hotel Fredonia Convention Center to celebrate the church's anniversary. The two living former pastors, Dr. Lionel Crowell and Dr. Bill Austin, attended with their wives. Pastors attending, left to right, were Dr. Allen Reed, Dr. Lionel Crowell, and Dr. Bill Austin. *Photo by Jimmy Partin.*

where he could "really get to know and love the people," put down roots, and provide stability for both the church and his family. He is gratified that he has been privileged to stand on the shoulders of the pastors who preceded him at First Baptist Church and build on what they accomplished. Among the challenges he sees facing First Baptist Church are expanding the church's sphere of influence in reaching lost people and effectively ministering to the congregation through worship, Bible teaching, and programs. He feels that the church must remain focused on its mission and not be distracted by denominational politics; that the congregation, and all Christians, must take a strong stance on the importance of the traditional

Pastors' wives are an integral part of their ministry. The wives of pastors attending the 125th Anniversary banquet were, left to right, Mary Frances Fickett, Shirley (Graves) Bailey, Margie Austin, Mary Alice Crowell, and Linda Reed. *Photo by Jimmy Partin.*

family, adhere to Biblical standards of morality, maintain our American freedom to worship without government interference, and confront the threat of radical Islamists to world security.

When Reed and his wife were in college and dating, they traveled through Nacogdoches on their way to visit her parents in Conroe, Texas. Passing by First Baptist Church, Reed commented, "Wouldn't it be nice to be pastor of a church like that?"[9] Twenty-two years later Reed became the pastor of the church and embarked with the congregation on a journey of building the body of believers known as First Baptist Church of Nacogdoches. During his ministry at First Baptist Church, Reed has endeared himself to the congregation through his love for his flock, his sense of humor, and his Bible-based preaching. It is Reed's hope that First Baptist Church will continue to have a vision of reaching the Nacogdoches community for Christ, ministering to people of all ages, keeping pace with the times, and being a lighthouse that makes a difference locally and throughout the world.

Rick Warren, pastor of Saddleback Valley Community Church in Lake Forest, California, defines success for a pastor as "loving and leading consistently."[10] For twenty-eight years Dr. Allen Reed has consistently loved and led the congregation of First Baptist Church. May the journey he began with the congregation in 1981 continue many more years.

Vignettes depicting the 1880s, 1940s, and the present were part of the 125th Anniversary banquet. Dramatizing the period of the church's founding are, left to right, Laura Dunn, Quentin Risner, Marlon McDonald, and Amber Riggs. *Photo by Jimmy Partin.*

"[THE CHURCH] IS LIKE YOUR FAMILY. WHEN YOU BELONG TO A CHURCH AND HAVE A CHURCH FAMILY, YOU ARE NEVER ALONE."

Mary Frances (Dorsey) Fickett

1. Pastor Search Committee, Dr. George Thompson, Chairman to the Members of First Baptist Church, January 26, 1981.

2. Mary Cunningham, Notes on Dr. Allen Reed, January 1984.

3. Allen Reed, Biographical Sketch, unpublished, undated MS in the archives of the First Baptist Church Nacogdoches.

4. Ibid.

5. Allen Reed, Sermon Notes for March 1, 1981.

6. Anecdote relayed by Allen Reed.

7. Jimmy Partin, Personal Notes on 1984 FBC Centennial Celebration Banquet.

8. David Reed, video interview with Jean Rudisill, April 30, 2008.

9. Allen Reed, interview with Jimmy Partin, January 3, 2009.

10. Rick Warren, *The Purpose Driven Church* (Grand Rapids, MI: Zondervan Press, 1995), p. 26.

Epilogue

Those Who Come Behind Us

"May all who come behind us find us faithful."

Jon Mohr

> "FIRST BAPTIST HAS ALWAYS BEEN A LIGHT THAT SHINES FOR JESUS IN NACOGDOCHES. IF WE CONTINUE TO SERVE OUR SAVIOR, IF WE KEEP OUR EYES TO THE PATH THAT THE HOLY SPIRIT WOULD HAVE US FOLLOW, AND IF WE SERVE OTHERS BY SHARING THE LOVE OF GOD WITH THEM, I BELIEVE THAT GOD WILL CONTINUE TO BLESS THIS CHURCH."
>
> *Christine (Mrs. C. S.) Jones*

IN A RECENT ISSUE OF THE *BAPTIST STANDARD* PUBLISHED BY THE BAPTIST General Convention of Texas, Randel Everett, executive director of the BGCT Executive Board, complimented the state's 1,193 Baptist churches that are more than one hundred years old and stated that they have a significant impact on the convention, giving birth to many of the younger churches. "Many of our older congregations continue to provide wisdom and leadership for our newer churches. Pastors and staff have come and gone. Some have brought energetic ideas, others wise pastoral counseling. Some led with bright theological clarity, and others may have caused divisions and mistrust. They have survived economic, political, social and theological challenges. Yet these churches have continued to provide a Christian witness in their communities . . . [and] they often provide stability to associations and Baptist institutions . . . Our BGCT family is blessed because we have [both] new and seasoned churches. As we seek to understand our future, we would be wise to listen to the churches that weathered storms and found ways to reconnect with communities that always have been changing."[1] Everett was speaking on the occasion of the 130th anniversary of the First Baptist Church of Corpus Christi, but he could just as easily have been speaking about First Baptist Church of Nacogdoches on its 125th anniversary.

First Baptist Church has weathered many storms in the past 125 years. There have been times with financial challenges, times when there were disagreements among members or between pastor and members, and times when doctrinal controversies within the denomination threatened. Always, however, the members of First Baptist Church have sought to fulfill the church's mission of:

- Finding the lost, wherever they may be, and sharing with them the good news of salvation through faith in Jesus Christ,

- Building the believer through preaching the Word, Bible study, and fellowship,

- Changing the world by witnessing and ministering in Christ's name wherever their life and work has taken them.

The future will have storms and challenges of its own. Times continue to change. As in the past, forms of worship are changing. There are new music genres. Technology is changing the way people learn and communicate. The stresses of modern life create new needs and opportunities for ministry. However, regardless of what changes and challenges occur, the believers known as First Baptist Church of Nacogdoches, Texas, can face them confident that the God and Savior they serve never changes; He is the same yesterday, today, and forever. Knowing this, they can face the future confident that they can meet any challenge that may come their way.

In 1988, Jon Mohr penned the following words:

Oh may all who come behind us find us faithful.
May the fire of our devotion light their way.
May the footsteps that we leave,
Lead them to believe,
And the lives we live inspire them to obey.
Oh may all who come behind us find us faithful.[2]

The past 125 years have been a testimony to the faithfulness of those members of First Baptist Church of Nacogdoches who have gone before. When the next 125 years have passed, should the Lord tarry that long, may those who celebrate the church's 250th anniversary still be able to say that First Baptist Church is a faithful witness to the saving power of Jesus Christ.

---

1. Randel Everett, "Congratulations, First Baptist Church Corpus Christi," *The Baptist Standard*, September 1, 2008, p. 5.

2. Jon Mohr, "Find Us Faithful." Birdwing Music/ Jonathan Mark Music, 1988.

First Baptist Church Centennial Symbol

In 1984, First Baptist Church celebrated the centennial of its founding and a logo was created to commemorate this event. The symbol chosen for the logo was the triquetra, a centuries-old western symbol for eternity. Each of the three parts of the triquetra is composed of two curved intersecting lines that meet at a point radiating outward. These points, or visecas, are ancient symbols for the glory of God. Each curved line represents a member of the Trinity. Together they form the outline of a fish, another ancient symbol for Christianity. The date of 1884 shows the year that First Baptist Church was founded, and the phrase "Advancing the Kingdom of God" expresses the reason for the church's existence. In adopting this logo for its centennial celebration, the church adopted this statement: "It is hoped that this symbol will be used, not only during the Centennial Celebration, but always, for there will never come a time when our church will have any other purpose but to advance the Kingdom of God through Jesus Christ our Lord." *First Baptist Church Archives.*

Appendix A: Statement of Purpose
First Baptist Church
Nacogdoches, Texas

Statement of Purpose

First Baptist Church of Nacogdoches, Texas, is a ministering body of Jesus Christ. Guided by the Holy Spirit, our purpose is to proclaim and practice the Christian life as revealed in God's Holy Word.

Therefore, we are committed to:

Joyfully participating within the Body of Christ
- By worship and praise to God (Psalm 100)
- By the study of His written word (II Timothy 2:15)
- By the observance of the church ordinances (Matthew 28:19; I Corinthians 11:24–25)
- By persistent prayer (I Thessalonians 5:17)
- By the exercise of our spiritual gifts (I Corinthians 12)
- By tithing of God's abundance to us (Malachi 3:10)

Unselfishly sharing with others
- Spiritually: The good news of Jesus Christ (I Corinthians 1:23–24)
- Materially: Our possessions (Matthew 25: 31–46)
- Personally: Our time, concern, love, and acceptance (Luke 10:25–37)

Actively growing in the grace and knowledge of Jesus Christ
- By becoming more mature Christians (Hebrews 6:1–3)
- By discipling others within the body of Christ (Matthew 28:19–20)

Adopted April 12, 1992; Reaffirmed January 11, 1998

Appendix B: Pastors of First Baptist Church

1884–1886	Luther Rice Scruggs	1914–1919	Cornelius Albert Westbrook
1886–1890	William Gaddy	1920–1922	Samuel David Dollahite
1891–1893	Adoniram Judson Holt	1923–1939	Bonnie Grimes
1893–1896	Herman Boerhave Pender	1939–1942	Jared I. Cartlidge
1896–1897	Thomas Bunyan Harrell	1943–1951	Lifus Earl Lamb
1897–1899	Albert Bell Vaughn Jr.	1951–1954	Jared I. Cartlidge
1900–1902	William Thomas Tardy	1954–1960	William H. Crook
1902–1905	Adoniram Judson Holt	1961–1967	W. Edwin Crawford
1905–1907	Aaron John Miller	1967–1972	Robert G. Graves
1908–1909	Roe Thomas Holleman	1972–1974	Bill R. Austin
1909–1910	Joseph Warren Bates	1974–1980	Paul Lionel Crowell
1911–1914	Thomas Coleman Mahan	1981–Present	Charles Allen Reed

Appendix C: Deacon Body
First Baptist Church
2008

Active Deacons

Doyle Alexander	Joe Biggerstaff	Jim Coats
Tom Atchison	Jerry Blackmon	Tom Davis
Steve Barber	Jimmy Carpenter	Roger Driggers
	Richard Chambers	Larry Duett

Bradley Durham
Jack Erwin
Dennis Fleetwood
Dale Frost
Tommy Fuller
John Gayler
Bill Goodrum
Russ Hairston
Tip Harris
Durward Henry
Kevin Jones
Ricky Jones
Langston Kerr
Ira Lawson
David Mackey
Craig Matson
Mike McClellan
Bill McWhorter
Bennat Mullen
Jimmy Partin
Richard Partin
Dale Perritt

Charles Pool
Ed Pool
James Prince
Johnny Rudisill
David Russell
Neolin Shiller
Jim Shipp
Mark Simmons
Bill Simms
Jack Sinz
Ken Smith
Nick Southers
Wesley Taylor
Ron Theiss
Robert Van Norman
J. B. Watson
Art Wheeless
John Woods
Jimmie Yeiser
John Young
Leon Young

Reserve Deacons
Terry Bell
Buck Fausett
Jeff Hamilton
Guy Howard
Stanley Jones
Richard Tallent
Dan Walker
Don Wyatt

Emeritus Deacons
William (Bill) Duke (Deceased–
    December 1, 2008)
Dee Jones
Billy Muckleroy
Jimmie Simms
Clois Walker
Ray Young

Appendix D: Financial History

The financial records of First Baptist Church prior to the 1950s are sketchy, probably as a result of the fires in 1952 and 1953. For financial information on the church's early years, one must rely on the annual reports of the local Baptist association and W. T. Parmer's *Seventy-five Years in Nacogdoches: A History of the First Baptist Church, 1884–1959* (Dallas: Dorsey Co., 1959).

From records available it appears that there was no formally adopted budget for the church prior to the mid-1930s. Before that time, the church relied on weekly offerings collected during Sunday services. Whenever collections were insufficient to pay the pastor's salary, the church treasurer called on members and solicited additional contributions to make up the difference. Existing financial records from this period show expenditures only. From 1911 to 1922, church expenditures, as reported by Parmer, were:

1911	$2,765	**1918**	No record
1912	$3,902	**1919**	$2,696
1913	$4,303	**1920**	$3,746
1914	$2,375	**1921**	$10,382
1915	$2,753	**1922**	$8,484
1916	$5,578	**1923–1949**	No records
1917	$4,826		

In the fall of 1935, the Reverend Bonnie Grimes led the congregation to begin financing the church through an adopted budget underwritten by pledges from the membership. The budget system of church finance is still used by the congregation, but the practice of asking members to pledge a specific amount to underwrite the annual budget has been discontinued. In recent years, pledges have been solicited only for building programs and specific projects.

During the last half of the twentieth century, the budget grew rapidly. The budget of 2000 for $1,266,341 was 29.9 times the budget for 1950 of $42,320, an increase of almost 3,000 percent. The most rapid growth during this period occurred in the decade between 1970 and 1980, when the budget increased by almost a half million dollars, from $183,326 to $643,973. Much of this increase, however, was due to including loan payments on the Christian Life Center debt in the budget. The budget, by decades, from 1950 to 2009, was as follows:

1950	$42,320
1960	$115,420
1970	$183,326
1980	$643,973
1990	$923,308
2000	$1,266,341
2009	$1,979,191

These amounts do not include designated gifts, special offerings for missions, love offerings for guest preachers and staff anniversaries, or other special collections. In addition, the congregation has for several decades designated 10 percent of the budget for the Southern Baptist Convention's Cooperative Program that supports Baptist missionaries, schools, and hospitals as well as the Convention's programs and staff. When total budget receipts exceed the budget, the church sends 10 percent of the money actually received for the budget to the Cooperative Program.

Appendix E: Church Plant and Facilities

Most evangelical Christians would agree that the New Testament definition of "the church" refers not to the building or place of meeting, but to a congregation of believers. Still the facility in which a specific church meets tends to be the focal point for any body of believers in a community. If asked the location of the First Baptist Church, the average person on the streets of Nacogdoches would probably refer to the church plant at 411 North Street, not to the body of believers dispersed to their jobs and homes in the city. As the focal point of a specific congregation in the community, and as the location of a large number of the activities of its members, a church's facilities tend to be the most visible representation of its presence, and they play a significant role in the achievement of its mission.

The story of First Baptist Church's facilities is the story of the church's efforts to provide a place where members of the congregation and guests can meet for worship, study, and fellowship—a place where the body finds empowerment to live, work, and witness in the larger community.

From the beginnings of First Baptist, its facilities have occupied a prominent and highly visible location on the west side of North Street, approximately four blocks north of the Nacogdoches County Courthouse and the downtown business district. When Luther Rice Scruggs began Baptist missionary work in Nacogdoches in 1884, he reported that the most pressing need of the twenty-six professing Baptists he found in the community was a place to meet and hold services. By the end of 1885, the thirteen charter members of the congregation had purchased a lot at 411 North Street from Julia Curl and Anna M. and J. C. Shindler and constructed a small, wood-frame church. The total cost for both lot and building was $950. This little white frame structure served as the congregation's place of worship for fourteen years.

By 1899, the congregation had outgrown the original building, and a decision was made to replace the building with a new, larger place of worship that would include rooms for Sunday school, an office for the pastor, and a kitchen. Diedrich Rulfs, a German immigrant and Nacogdoches' premier architect at the time, designed the structure. The Gothic-style building he envisioned was constructed on the site of the original church and cost $13,000.

In 1928, the congregation had grown to the point that the old building could no longer accommodate its members, especially for Sunday school, and plans were begun for a new, larger building. Before these plans could be carried out, however, the Great Depression intervened and the congregation settled for constructing a three-story, brick educational annex at the rear of the frame church designed by Rulfs. John Hamlin was the contractor for the annex. It was completed in 1932 at a cost of $18,000.

By 1942, in spite of wartime shortages of building materials, the congregation was able to build a new sanctuary. The old wooden building was demolished and the new brick structure erected on the same site and joined to the previously constructed three-story educational annex. This red-brick colonial-style building was completed in 1942, with cash and pledges of $12,000 and a $30,000 loan from the M. A. Anderson Foundation in Houston, Texas. The architect was Hal Tucker of Nacogdoches, and John Hamlin was the contractor. In 2009, this building remains the central portion and main sanctuary of the church plant. During this period the congregation began acquiring parcels of adjoining property as they became available, and by 2009, the church site extended from north of Baxter Duncan Street southward almost to Hospital Street and west from North Street to Taylor Avenue.

A fire in October 1952 left smoke and water damage to the interior. Only a few months after repairs had been completed, a second fire on July 1, 1953, gutted the interior of the sanctuary, leaving only the four walls standing. Plans that had been underway for expanding the church's educational space were put on hold until the sanctuary could be rebuilt. At this time the flat roof of the destroyed sanctuary was replaced with a pitched roof and a steeple was added. Once that had been accomplished, the congregation immediately began the previously planned expansion, adding the two-story north and south wings, a fellowship hall, and a chapel. Nacogdoches architect Hal Tucker was the designer and J. A. Nesbit was the contractor for rebuilding the sanctuary. Ellis Kingham and Son were contracted for the expansion that was completed in 1955. Except for maintenance and minor remodeling, this was the last major building project for the congregation until the stained glass windows were installed in the sanctuary in 1970.

In keeping with trends in programming for evangelical churches and to better meet the total needs of the church family, the congregation added the Christian Life Center to the rear of the north wing in 1978 at a cost of $1.5 million. The Christian Life Center provided an expanded kitchen, ceramics and hobby rooms, a gymnasium, a racquetball court, a bowling alley, and space for table games. In addition to the Christian Life Center, a one-story, early childhood building was constructed west of the south wing. It provided space for nursery and preschool divisions as well as Day School classes. Interior remodeling of the ground floor of the south wing at this time expanded the office space to accommodate the growing church staff. Don Tew of Austin, Texas, was the architect, and Nacogdoches contractor and First Baptist Church member Tom Evans was the contractor.

To provide better access to the building during inclement weather, a porte cochere and parking lot were added to the north wing in 1996, and another porte cochere was added to the south wing in 1999.

The last addition to the church's physical plant was the three-story Children's Building. It incorporated the existing preschool building and provided educational space for children from bed babies through elementary school, a dedicated room for children's church, plus Sunday school space for the children's parents. This building was completed in 2005 at a cost of $4.5 million. Hatfield and Holcomb, Architects, of Dallas, Texas, were the designers, and J. E. Kingham Construction Company of Nacogdoches was the contractor. As part of their services designing the Children's Building, the architect developed a master site plan for the church's property and identified possible locations for future expansions of the church plant, such as a new sanctuary and parking lots.

Although not the "church," but only the place where the members of First Baptist Church meet to study and worship, the congregation's physical plant, in its prominent location on North Street, is a witness—a witness that for 125 years an active body of Baptist believers in the saving grace of Jesus Christ has met and worshipped on the site.

Selected Bibliography

Primary Sources:

The most significant primary sources for the history of First Baptist Church of Nacogdoches, Texas, are minutes of church conferences, minutes of the church's deacon body, the church's financial records, and the church's annual reports to the Shelby-'Doches Baptist Association. It should be noted, however, that few church records exist from prior to the 1950s. There are some handwritten minutes and copies of church rolls dating to the 1930s and 1940s, but there are almost no extant records prior to that time. This lack of early church records may be due to the fires that destroyed parts of the building in 1952 and 1953. Equally important are the personal memories of members of the congregation contained in letters and in interviews conducted for the church's one-hundredth-anniversary celebration in 1984, and for the one-hundred-twenty-fifth-anniversary celebration in 2009. These, and the other official records of the church, are housed in the church archives.

Other helpful unpublished sources include A. W. Birdwell, "Historical Sketch of the First Baptist Church of Nacogdoches" (MS in the Archives of First Baptist Church of Nacogdoches, Texas), 1945; Mildred Sitton, "The Physical Growth and Expansion of First Baptist Church, Nacogdoches, Texas, 1884–1977" (MS in the Archives of First Baptist Church of Nacogdoches, Texas), 1977; James G. Partin, "Speech for Daughters of the Republic of Texas Luncheon" (MS in possession of the author), 1983; and the First Baptist Church Scrapbooks—four volumes of material compiled by a committee chaired by Diane (Reese) Jones for the Centennial Celebration of First Baptist Church in 1984.

Additional unpublished material and photographs are in the East Texas Research Center of the Ralph W. Steen Library on the campus of Stephen F. Austin State University.

Secondary Sources:

The most important secondary source for the history of First Baptist Church is, without doubt, William Tellis Parmer's *Seventy-five Years in Nacogdoches: A History of the First Baptist Church, 1884–1959* (Dallas: Dorsey Co., 1959), published as part of the congregation's celebration of its seventy-fifth anniversary. Many of the sources Parmer consulted are no longer available to researchers, and his book is the only source for the information they provided. Adoniram Judson Holt's *Pioneering in the Southwest* (Nashville: The Sunday School Board of the Southern Baptist Convention, 1923) is especially helpful in researching the church's beginnings, and Miriam McConnell Lamb's *Our Years Together* (privately published, 1976) provides insight into the pastorate of the Reverend L. E. Lamb. Carolyn Reeves Ericson's *Fires and Firemen of Nacogdoches* (Nacogdoches, TX: Ericson Books, 1976) contains an excellent recounting of the two fires that destroyed the church in the 1950s. Willie Earl Woods Tindall's "Religion: Recollections and Reckonings" in *The Bicentennial Commemorative History of Nacogdoches* (Nacogdoches, TX: Nacogdoches Jaycees, 1976) is a good source for information on the establishment of religious institutions in Nacogdoches, and *Nacogdoches: The History of Texas' Oldest City* (Lufkin, Texas: Best of East Texas Publishers, 1995) by James G. Partin, Carolyn Reeves Ericson, Joe E. Ericson, and Archie McDonald is useful for the history of the city of Nacogdoches.

A considerable body of material on the history of First Baptist Church appears in numerous articles in the Nacogdoches *Daily Sentinel*, and the *Baptist Standard*, published by the Baptist General Convention of Texas, contains some helpful articles on the church and Texas Baptists in general.

Index

About the Author

James (Jimmy) G. Partin is retired from the Nacogdoches Independent School District where he served as teacher, principal, central office administrator, and superintendent. He is currently a lecturer of social studies methods in

 the Department of Elementary Education of Stephen F. Austin State University. Partin co-authored *Nacogdoches: The History of Texas' Oldest City* in 1995 with Carolyn Reeves Ericson, Joe E. Ericson, and Archie McDonald. He grew up in Nacogdoches attending First Baptist Church. With the exception of a brief sojourn as a member of Hyde Park Baptist Church in Austin, Texas, while in graduate school at the University of Texas, he has been a member of First Baptist Church, Nacogdoches, since his conversion in 1948. He resides in Nacogdoches with his wife, Peggy Doss Partin, who also grew up attending First Baptist Church. They are the parents of two daughters, Melanie Partin Matson and Amy Partin Durham, and grandparents of four grandchildren, all of whom reside in Nacogdoches and attend First Baptist Church.